Invisibility Toolkit

Lance Henderson

Table of Contents

Preface

Burn Notice and Skip Tracers

    A World Wide Web of Deceit

    Aliases

    IP Address Searches

    The Courts

    How to Knit A Cloak of Invisibility

    How to Create an Anonymous Bank Account

    Bitcoins

Student Loans

    Tax Offsets

    Prevention: Higher Education's Worst Enemy

    Consolidation, IBR and Forgiveness

Social Security Numbers

    Employment

    Things to Avoid

        Universities

        Labs

Dorms

Changing Your Name

White Lies

Clone Home

Passports & Canada

Anonymous Phones

How the FBI Traces Calls

Cons of Using a Burner

Pros of Using a Burner

Disappearing from Social Media

Phase 1: Nuking the Sites From Orbit

Phase 2: Nuking Criminal and Public Records

Phase 3: Staying Off The Radar

Stalkers

The Bayou Grandma Stalker

Willy Wonka Stalker Factory

The Hitchhiker

Ruin Her Life!

Securing Your Computer

Tor

Tails

Vpns

Freenet

Frost

Counter-Forensics

Truecrypt

Drivecrypt

Veracrypt

DiskCryptor

LibreCrypt

CIA Manipulation and Disappearing

Manipulation Tactics

Forging Alliances

Yuri Bezmenov

How The NSA Finds Anyone

Predictability

Cell Towers

Drones (and How to Defeat Them)

Bin Laden's Courier and the Art of Staying Invisible

Risky Friendships

Snowden's Mistakes

Defeating Facial Recognition Technology

College Dorms

Going To Extremes

Philippines

Pinays

Employment

Property

Cost of Living

Visas

Embassies

Police

Street Kids

Dodging the Bullet

Canada

Escape from New York

Sanctuaries

Canadian Border Officers and Encrypted Laptops

Cons of Canada

Cost of Living

Montreal

Money

Poisoning the Old Self

Thailand

Cost of Living

Safety Issues

Opsec in Thailand

Offline Opsec

Online Opsec

China

Disappearing Behind the Great Wall

Hong Kong Rudeness

Counterfeiting

The Final Disappearing Act

Final Thoughts

Other Books

Preface

Winston Churchill once said, "If you find yourself in Hell... keep going."

I can relate to that as easily as you can. But these days Hell itself seems to have taken on an altogether foreign form that's wholly different than the medieval version. These days, many 'angels of light' profess to know what's good for us better than we do ourselves - which is sheer lunacy.

We're not sheep. We all see it. We're not blind. And some of us want to act as beacons of light in a sea of darkness rather than go "Baaaaa!" like sheep to the bloody slaughter. We want to lead others away from the slaughterhouse. But to do that requires a specific set of skills that you don't learn in college.

Skills that will help us turn back the tide of Armageddon on individual sovereignty. Because let's face it, attacks on privacy have increased a thousand-fold. Every day new laws are passed that make privacy as rare as pink diamonds. In the future privacy may become as valuable as pink diamonds. Do you want to hear your grandkids ask you what it was like in the old days when people were *not* monitored 24/7?

Right. Didn't think so.

It's high-time we fought back and fought hard. If you've ever seen the Shawshank Redemption then you know what happens to weaklings - those that don't take action. They get raped again and again and again. Sooner or later you'll know the meaning of this phrase: "His judgment cometh and that right soon." It means war. Wouldn't you rather fight before the raping and pillaging starts? I would.

Judgment Day is already here. You cannot walk down the street without meeting a dozen street cams, and as an American-Canadian citizen there are times when I've wanted to disappear from society altogether. Vanish as though I'd slipped Frodo's elvish cloak over my neck and smoothed that runic ring right down my middle finger before flipping off the elites in power.

But first, a little story.

A story way back in 2001.

Living in close proximity to the housing projects of New Orleans, most days driving back from the University of New Orleans were uneventful. For the most part. Only Mardi Gras seemed to break the monotony along with eating soggy beignets (powdered donuts) on Bourbon Street.

Except for one day in particular while sweating in Manila-like traffic. On that day something terrifying happened. I decided to take a shortcut which turned out to be a shortcut into trouble. Before I knew it, a fourteen-year-old girl, black with ripped jeans, red sweatshirt and a nose that could put a bloodhound to shame ran in front of my beat-up Camaro while I drove 15MPH.

I slammed on the brakes and missed her hip by an inch. She slammed her fists on the hood of my car. Boom. Then she flipped me off real casual like this sort of thing happened every time it rained. I hopped out, furious, and proceeded to make sure she knew how close she'd come to a date with the grim reaper.

A cacophony of yelling ensued with every color of the rainbows. Soft swearing, hard swearing, and sweating (mostly me) as she matched every curse word with one better, more deviant, and fueled with twice the rage as though she'd been bred for no other reason than to unleash it all on me on that fiery summer day. A vampiric Lady Macbeth, this thug was. But none of that really mattered to the law. No sir, what mattered was when I grabbed her arm and stabbed a finger into her face as I shouted to be more careful. I began to walk away.

Only I wasn't going anywhere.

Her brother came running. A BIG brother wearing a dozen gold chains and carrying a chain big enough to tie a velociraptor. I swear the guy looked straight out of the A-Team. After that, her mother came screaming and what I presumed at the time was her grandmother, broom in hand (a witch?). I panicked as the big brother threw me to the ground as mama called the cops. I remember expecting a black cat to come along any minute to scratch my face to shreds. I was going down in flames though I was innocent of any abuse.

Fast-forward three weeks later and I'm having my ass handed to me by the most militant judge I'd ever laid eyes on. A real man hater whose harpy-like claws seemed to grow the more I sweat. I had only one choice: Play along. So I kissed ass like I'd never done before in my whole miserable life. At the end of her screeching rant, I ended up getting off on a technicality. The police had screwed up somewhere, it seemed.

My record was as clean as a babe's arse. Clear as crystal.

Or so I thought. Later that year, a detective came knocking. It seemed that the little girl had disappeared, and to my horror it turned out that he knew everything about *me*. Things that were not in the court transcript. Things I'd done were recorded by various cameras set up around the city. The entire city seemed to be turning a shade Orwellian.

"Talk to me," he said smiling with that shiny badge gleaming. I frowned. Talk to the cops? "Yeah," he replied. "Talk to me or get put on the sex offender's list for abusing that little girl."

Abuse?

I clammed up. Granted, I was naive, but not stupid. He ended up letting me go after throwing down every threat imaginable. After that I wanted to vanish even more, and as I would later learn, I wasn't the first to go through such an ordeal.

Up until that point, I'd always trusted the police, or for that matter any kind of higher authority in government. I trusted the media. I trusted newspapers. I trusted juries.

About the only thing I never trusted were the palm readers who always set up shop around the French Quarter.

Well, no longer.

From that point on, I swore to myself I'd learn how to be invisible, or die trying. True, I escaped the sex offender registry by keeping my mouth shut. Others have not been so lucky. I've heard another author (Wendy McElroy) relate a similar story:

"Last summer, an Illinois man lost an appeal on his conviction as a sex offender for grabbing the arm of a 14-year-old girl. She had stepped directly in front of his car, causing him to swerve in order to avoid hitting her.

Fitzroy Barnaby was 28 years old. He jumped out his car, grabbed her arm and lectured her on how not to get killed. Nothing more occurred. Nevertheless, that one action made him guilty of "the unlawful restraint of a minor," which is a sexual offense in Illinois. Both the jury and the judge believed him. Nevertheless, Barnaby went through years of legal proceedings that ended with his name on a sex offender registry, where his photograph and address were publicly available. He must report to authorities. His employment options are severely limited; he cannot live near schools or parks."

Here I was thinking I was the only guy that had experienced such a horrific day. The absurd part is not even that it happened. It's that it is never forgiven. It's never put in the past where mistakes are buried. They are broadcast forever, branded over and over into our memories. Forgiveness, that is, granting your past actions invisible to everyone but you and the Almighty, is outlawed.

Well. This book aims to reverse that trend. It aims to give you back your privacy and if you need it, **invisibility**.

You don't want newspaper reporters sticking mics in your face before you've had your day in court do you? This happened to me. I remember feeling like I'd killed everyone's favorite rock star.

Think on how your life would change if this happened to you:

• Someone uses your unsecured WiFi to threaten the President.

• A hacker steals your credit card to buy Russian child porn using proxies.

• You hear sirens just as your phone rings. You pick up to hear a TV reporter asking for an interview since you were the last person to see the Governor alive at the Beau Chene Country Club - who was later found dead in a pool of blood in the restroom - the same one you used.

• The powers that be are coming after you for child support - without allowing you to see your own children. You try to visit Canada to "get away from it all" for a while, when you are *arrested* at the border. Things get worse when they find a few "manga" comics in your back seat. Manga that is illegal in Canada but not the USA. Chaos ensues. They rip your reputation apart in the name of *the law*.

• Your ten year old brother jokes to his pals on the school yard that he has a shed full of Rambo-like grenades and a few barrels of gunpowder. A girl overhears. She snitches. The cop arrest *him* (not kidding) but later let him go. Years later, that report shows up when he tries to join the Marines. He is *rejected*. Yes, this really happened to a relative in Louisiana. And that's not to say Louisiana is any better or worse than any other state where hysteria can run amok and drag you along for the ride. The fact is, I'll show you how to prevent crap like this from happening no matter which country you are in.

If you are ever investigated, the authorities will likely tear your place apart looking for anything to build a solid case to hand to the prosecutor. Who knows what your situation might be at that time. You might need to go away for a while to strategize with attorneys, maintain your business, speak to family, move assets, etc. It is difficult to do that from a jail cell.

The USA now has a "guilty until proven innocent" legal system. You are not innocent until proven guilty, but I will teach you how to gain that precious commodity called TIME which you can use to gather resources to defend yourself. Resources that go well with becoming **invisible**.

You will learn:

1.) How to be anonymous *offline* as well as on.

2.) How to use your surroundings to lessen risk, special forces style.

3.) How to detect when you are being data-mined: How to hide where you went to school, where you've lived, whom you've loved, whom you did not. Your shopping habits, dating habits, political affiliations. You get the picture.

4.) How to look like a small fish and not a BIG FISH.

And that's just the beginning.

Burn Notice and Skip Tracers

Burn Notice is one of my favorite TV shows. I don't watch much TV but I do if that show is on. I'd stop to watch it even if a mugger came in and stuck me in the ribs before making off with my wallet. It's that grand. It's thrilling. It's top notch espionage and underground battle-of-the-wits style American James Bond. Sort of like True Lies but with better looking agents.

In case you haven't seen it, let me describe it for you. The 'burn notice' itself usually comes from an intelligence agency, but can be from any alphabet agency really. It doesn't even need to be on paper. You can get 'The Call' while on a mission in Iran or Brazil or Eastern Europe. What happens is this: The CIA calls you up and at the most inopportune moment tells you they wish to 'wash their hands of you'.

You're done. You're cooked. You're career as an agent is finished.

They cut the umbilical quick and every connection to an agent is severed in true Mission: Impossible fashion. And all for what, you ask? Easy. So they can save face. Any agent has no idea what he did (well maybe a few might have an idea) but he knows he has no work history, no connections, no support and no cash. Poor guy is burned for good.

Well, sort of. If some bigwig at the FBI wants info on him, he can get it from said agency if he has enough pull and the person is a high-value target.

As I watched this show for years I kept thinking: Wouldn't it be great to give yourself your own 'Burn Notice'? Disappear from society altogether? Get a fresh start with new name, new job, the works, in some country where pretty Filipinas fall out of coconut trees as you sit on a beach drinking margaritas?

Well okay, maybe not *that* extravagant. Perhaps it's more simple for you. You want to keep the collector's off your back while you grow a business to pay back your student loans. Start a new relationship. Get away from an abusive wife wielding a double-bladed axe.

It's all rather easy to speculate but difficult to implement. We like our safety nets. We like our 'safe jobs', and a lot of guys don't like losing money in online ventures. So they play it safe. They refuse to take risks. Then one day when they need to leave the country, they can't because they took no action.

Then there are skip tracers to worry about.

What're those, they ask? From wiki.

Skip tracing tactics may be employed by debt collectors, process servers, bail bond enforcers (bounty hunters), repossession agents, private investigators, attorneys, police detectives, and journalists, or by any person attempting to locate a subject whose contact information is not immediately known. Similar techniques have also been utilized by investigators to locate witnesses in a criminal trial.

Before we deal with skip tracers, a word of caution: NEVER fake your own death or disappearance since doing so will bring more heat on you than if you shot Dirty Harry in the ass. Even a simple disappearance can lead to a statewide manhunt, or womanhunt in the case of Leanne Bearden who after a 2-year globe-trotting vacation vanished one hot Texas day.

"I'm going for a walk. Be back in one hour!" were her last words.

She hanged herself from a tree in a wooded area close to her in-laws home. Police helicopters, dogs, and even state troopers spent hundreds of hours looking for her (no suicide note), fearing she'd been snatched and kidnapped. I sat stunned at all the Youtube comments calling for the husband's crucifixion, and all without any evidence he'd done anything.

Don't do this.

Don't kill yourself over bad debts. Don't do it over unemployment (apparently why the woman hanged herself). Don't do it over a failed marriage (taken the Red Pill, yet?). Don't fake your own death and try to buy fake IDs from Craigslist. If you try to cross the Canadian border with a fake passport (because we know how nice those border officers are on the Fourth of July with a thousand Canadian-made cars in line to shop), and that one guard can ban you for life. Ask George Bush what happened when one tries to cross with a DUI record. He had to get a waiver. But more on this later.

Instead, what we want to do is plant false leads that end in Nowheresville for any Skip Tracer hot on your trail. That's what the next few chapters are about. Getting somewhere while leading any skip tracer or other investigator to believe they're on a wild good chase.

A World Wide Web of Deceit

Your most prized tool in seeking information is also your enemy's most prized tool for seeking your loss of freedom be it handcuffs, garnishments or even asset forfeiture, to which the ATF has turned into a profit-industry. Your neck is out there online as naked as the day you were born.

Being the smart cookie you are, you know it isn't rocket science to vanish online. Lots of guides explain how to cloak your identity using all kinds of tools. Tor for starters. Most computer literate people know of it. Then there is chatting on Freenet. That's not so easy. Then there are VPNs that hide your IP address. You can even chain proxies to post encrypted messages on Usenet with them if you know how to buy services anonymously.

But those guides rarely tell you what pops up when a seasoned skip tracer simply keys in your home phone number or alias into a search engine and starts calling every person you've ever known. That's the part even the encryption experts forget about: That which is right under their very noses. Tracers, like collections, will harass everyone on your city block about you. And boy do they lie. They lie with more skill than the Devil himself!

Aliases

Let's talk about aliases. I'd bet good money that you or your kids use the same alias on Facebook and Twitter that you do on Usenet and The Pirate Bay, or some combination thereof. Maybe something cool like Windsong. You'll switch it up a bit on other sites, maybe go by Windsinger or some such. Oh there might be an extra number or two here and there, but we humans are creatures of habit. We don't like hard work and having multiple *different* aliases for every social media... well some of us just cannot be bothered because that's too much work for us to do. Mistake numero uno.

To prove a point to one of my beautiful nieces in Louisiana, I had her type in a nic she uses on Twitter and P2P. It wasn't just her P2P messages that popped up but those she'd typed on Usenet as well - messages from long dormant times when she was a wee pre-teen. As it turned out, Google indexes Usenet messages from decades ago. I almost felt bad for showing her Usenet at such a young age. And believe me, most of us Usenet guys back then never in a million years believed we'd have a 7 year retention rate offered by Usenet farms.

But the real danger was using that same nic across the board on several social media sites.

One website allows you to look up people based on name alone. We found a dozen, yes... a dozen Americans in the south with the exact same name as her but not one with the same nic. Anywhere in social media.

The nick? LinuxGirl.

Any Skip Tracer worth his own salt might think she has a nerd gene (she does). She loves coding C++, Java, too. She loves The Matrix and adores the little blonde hacker geek from Jurassic Park like a long lost sister. Any Skip Tracer would find her messages sprawled across the net on every tech forum known to man. She's quite open about her age, too.

When we looked at all the info, it lead a trail right to her bedroom. So many years and so many clues built quite the profile. She freaked out as any red-headed teenager would but only because she feared they might find out which boy she has a crush on.

"Ye gods!" I snapped. "That's all you're worried about?" To which she replied, "What else could happen?"

We were even able to find out from these messages where she meets her fellow high school geeks for PvP Warcraft and Fallout marathons, the pen and paper game, not the PC RPG.

IP Address Searches

Be cautious about skipping privacy protection if you have an online business. Skip Tracers can execute a simple online WHOIS search that often reveals who owns the domain, which would be *you*. They may even gain your address. If they cannot find the domain owner outright, they may be able to follow clues you've left in your posts.

But you'd never be so careless to leave your real name, right?

Right... but the problem isn't you. The problem is *your relatives. Your friends. Your business associates.* Your ex-lovers. A clever Skip Tracer will lie to fish the info out of them.

And they always sugarcoat it, appearing as someone who wants to help you - an angel of light and niceness and puffy clouds: A prospective employer. A lawyer looking to give away inheritance money (yeah, right). A movie director who wants to offer you the role of a lifetime.

You may hear a lot of affiliate marketers say that it doesn't matter if you have WHOIS protection or not, but I disagree. If you want to shield yourself, and by extension, your freedom (the secret to happiness by the way), then you need to not leave a money trail to your front doorstep.

The Courts

Got a speeding ticket recently? That'll show up in a public court record. And those records are not difficult to get. Anything that happens on public, tax-funded roads is often available to any Joe Blow who wants it. That includes fender-benders, drug busts and well, anything that involves you pleading to a judge.

A big danger is privately owned property. That is, property that can be taken away from you by the IRS, the Dept of Education, or your Uncle Frick who works for the EPA.

Loose lips sink ships. Who else knows about the land but you? Relatives? Friends? How easily can a Skip Tracer contact them about your land--which they so desperately want to buy for a million dollars?

Worse, you might be tempted to put this land on a bank loan application as collateral. Don't do that either. Such things are available to the public eye. Not the account numbers mind you, but your name and address. If you want to be invisible, don't go taking your elvish cloak off in Mordor where any green-skinned orc can sniff you out and ambush you.

How to Knit Your Own Elvish Cloak of Invisibility

Knowledge is power. Or rather, knowledge is *potential* power. That's the crux of it alright, as collectors and skip tracers must rely on your ignorance. In fact they prefer you not know your rights so as to better fuel whatever fear tactics they employ.

Let's say you see the writing on the wall and in six months you will default on a student loan. You feel helpless. You know the collectors will be coming. You know the phone will be ringing. You know they'll be calling your employer to harass you and your friends, your family. So what can you do?

Allow me to sound like a broken record: Knowledge is power. They rely on your ignorance and assuming your lender won't work with you and your Ombudsman is fond of Houdini acts, there are a few steps you can take to minimize grief.

If your name/address is scattered over social media like pepper on eggs, then you need to remove it before the slime-skinned collectors get a hold of it.

- Study the FDCPA like your livelihood depends upon it, which it does. Know what they can get away with and what they can't. Remember, knowledge is power. If you wield it, they will respect it.

- Check your aliases. Are they the same on every social media website? Is your phone number visible? What about your email? Can a collector or any stranger for that matter view your private info on Facebook? How about Twitter? LinkedIn?

- This above all: ask for any debt or claim to be given in writing. Student loans? Ask for a copy of the promissory note. Often they will NOT have this information. They will give every deadbeat excuse in the world so as not to send it, and believe me friend I have heard it all.

"We don't have to send that." (and that's a lie)

"We'll send it next week." (Another lie. If that's true, ask her to send you a screenshot.)

"You need to setup an automated payment plan first." (BIG LIE)

Always contest the debt and never send a payment until you get that promissory note or bank loan with your signature.

Also, look into these and know what they cannot do:

The Gramm-Leach Act - Legislation that limits the abuse they can leave on your message machine. Many collectors don't pay heed to this at all. Call them on it!

Fair Debt Collection Practices Act

Telephone Consumer Protection Act

The double-edged sword in all of this is that saying: "Please do not call me again!" This does not work. You must issue this in writing to the bank. It's called a no-contact order. Sometimes it works, sometimes not.

A close friend of mine happened to secure a lucrative deal (by her standards anyway) as an extra on a movie set in Los Angeles. She was an extra with a few speaking lines. Not much to brag about down at Igor's bar but it was a good amount for a day's work: $500. As luck would have it, her effort to pay down her student loan went awry. The collector called her mother and a few friends and managed to get the number of someone on the set. Snakes are clever!

You can imagine what happened. The whole set had to stop filming to allow her to answer that stupid call. So never underestimate what these hucksters will do to your reputation, and prepare accordingly.

How to Create an Anonymous Bank Account

One wintery night when few were paying attention, the Canadian Parliament decided to pass a budget bill containing the single most wicked act of treason in western history.

It's name is FATCA (Short for FATCAT). Developed by President Obama, Harry Reid and Nancy Pelosi in 2010 with a fully compliant Democratic Congress, it's workings are the kind of thing a superpower might enact in a sanctimonious bill against a terrorist state like Iran or North Korea. Certainly not Canada.

And when you get right down to it, it is an act of financial war - mandating every bank in Canada fork over the financial information of *any* Canadian with US citizenship. It's passed to the Canadian Tax Service, then to the IRS - the same who demand all Canadians with U.S. citizenship to file and/or pay taxes to the US despite not ever living there.

Things like this are a slippery slope to civil wars and revolutions. Worse, the Canadian Parliament did not resist in selling out it's own people. One politician in Parliament claimed "We had no choice as we had thirty days to decide or face a 30% penalty on all investments in the USA."

In other words, they were "just following orders."

Where've we heard that before?

At any rate it seems that Big Brother is alive and well and Judas himself could not have orchestrated a sharper backstab. A few Canadians have filed a federal lawsuit to be sure, claiming it to be unconstitutional (it is), but even if the suit is successful and the law overturned, banks will not be in a hurry to revert the bank's systems because it is so expensive.

But make no mistake: If you are a US citizen, they want to know so as to rat you out to the IRS for not paying taxes in two countries. In essence, for not being a nice little lemming with wrists outstretched. This is a problem for those who love freedom, and by extension, happiness, to say nothing about those who love anonymity.

So then, the question is... how to remain anonymous *legally*?

It is not really possible to be 100% anonymous with post-9/11 financial systems without spending a ton of money to do it. So big crime syndicates like those in Russia and Mexico have such money, but you and I do not. Sometimes all that you can purport to accomplish is *pseudo-anonymity*, which is far cheaper unless you want to live like Jeremiah Johnson and trade bear hides and beaver pelts. There are some options, however.

DAS SAFE
Seit 1984

Anonyme & Legitime Fächer
Es gibt immer Dinge, die Sie nicht zu Hause aufbewahren sollten.

SAFE Wertfachvermietungs Ges.m.b.H.
Auerspergstrasse 1, A-1080 Wien, Austria
Tel.: +43-1-406 61 74, E-mail: info@dassafe.com
FN 80874 h, Handelsgericht Wien,
UID Nr. ATU54387408

If you want to hide valuables from a greedy spouse and do not mind tangible assets, look into opening an anonymous deposit box overseas. It's still technically an "account" but Das Safe, located in Vienna, does a good job of preserving your privacy and demand no ID from you. Bear in mind though that if you lose your key, it's tough to retrieve another one.

Also be aware that anything sitting in an overseas vault is not convenient. It's time-consuming to get it, sell it, convert it to gold or cash and retrieve it and all paying attention to leaving no financial trail. But then financial anonymity has never been cheap. You have to weigh the needs of an emergency to your need of invisibility.

Other Options:

Bitcoin

You can go the Bitcoin route and buy currency, but you will face stiff fees as Paypal is a high-risk method when the two are paired. And there is a tough learning curve if you're not good with computers. Nevertheless, there are guides that can walk you through it but Bitcoins are not anonymous by themselves.

Ptshamrock - Here you can buy an anonymous debit card and other items. They are legitimate and have been around for years. However they're not cheap, nor are they perfect. Blackhat marketers sometimes use them.

Ocra outfits offshore investments, trusts and foundations for, as they term it, "Wealth Protection" and "International Business". You may find they offer something you need.

As you can see, there are downsides to just about every facet of anonymous financial accounts. What we've not discussed is *accessing* any of those accounts online. This is dangerous and should be avoided. But... there are times when you simply must get access to an online account and be **secure** doing it. Here's how:

1. A VPN (Virtual Private Network). Trial versions abound. You need this to shield yourself from search engines, *not* the government. For that, use Tor. Buy the VPN, the price of which is usually under ten bucks, then install Tor.

2. Tails/Tor downloaded to a memory stick if you're truly paranoid. My Tor book gives details if you want lengthy

examples but this above all: Never reveal any personal data.

3. Anonymous Debit Card, Loadable. If you load the card with cash, you must not do so within your own town.

Student Loans

English majors, perhaps more than any other major (except Gender Studies), make up the bulk of criticism for student loan debt. It goes well beyond snide comments made at the office. Politicians have come out slandering liberal arts majors in general, but you never hear them criticize STEM degrees, nor do they mention how brutal those programs are when Professor Punjab wants to shrink his incoming Biology class by 85% to free up some research time.

"Why did you not study chemistry or engineering? Or go for an MBA? Maybe an M.D.?" they ask you.

Often, these stone-throwers neglect to do any research on these other STEM degrees. If they did they'd realize that they take out just as much, if not more debt than their liberal arts brethren. Automation coupled with outsourcing is making *every* degree irrelevant, some faster than others. Even medical students are graduating with $200,000 in student loan debt. That's debt that is neither dischargeable in bankruptcy nor easy to pay off as they:

- Garnish your wages (but not before slandering you before your work colleagues)
- Seize your assets
- Crucify your relationship with your employer

Now it's *everyone's* problem.

The main problem students face, and one we will eradicate, is this: How does one work off the debt without being terrorized? Better yet, how does one make a *fresh start* when they've absolutely exhausted all options save that of stringing themselves up from the nearest tree?

In short, how to disappear at least temporarily so you can grow a business that enables the paying off of the debt?

Any businessman will tell you, debt will **kill any business**. You might be chuckling to hear this, wondering if such a thing is even *possible* for an English major.

"Pay off a student loan to the tune of a hundred grand by... writing, you say? Impossible!"

It most certainly is possible. I know this because my brother did it, but not before teaching him how to keep those baying bloodhounds at bay. Knowledge is 80% of the battle. That is, how to fight back. I showed him. He showed *them*. And I will show *you*.

Tax Offsets

Unless you live in Canada, any federally defaulted student loan will likely result in a tax offset by the IRS if it isn't dealt with. Cutting off communication works only if you've got leverage. If not, they take your tax return unless you happen to be self-employed (more on that later). Worse than this is when you are garnished *and* get a tax offset. Let's first discuss what legal options you have.

A few points:

- Your spouse can have her tax return taken as well even if she did not cosign the loan. She *can* however file an injured spouse form and send it to the IRS. Not the best option.

- You can **challenge** the offset using this link: (https://www.myeddebt.com/borrower/topReviewNavigati on)

 It's difficult and for this to be successful you need to prove validity as to why the offset should not occur. Here are some valid reasons:

1.) You've already paid the debt prior to them kickstarting the offset
2.) You're disabled (not temporarily)
3.) You've recently claimed bankruptcy
4.) You view the debt as unenforceable

Real problems arise when people put off challenging it. They ignore all warning signs and only at the end realize how serious it is. Therefore, *prevention* is paramount if you want to avoid collection agencies.

Prevention: The Department of Education's Worst Enemy

Be aware that if you try to outsmart the Dept. of Education, you'll have a tough time of establishing a reputation for your business if you want to expand. That is, to borrow money. Anonymity will be your calling card and you'll always be looking over your shoulder if you're in the USA. Problem is, creditors you ask for money don't like anonymity. It may get so difficult that you are tempted to leave for Canada, either to take up a student visa, work visa or to seek permanent residency there.

Other digital nomads have done this and succeeded. They're all over the place in every sense of the word. Some work for Odesk and eLance while others go the affiliate route, but not without jumping major hoops. That should be the last resort since you don't want something preventing you from using your passport.

That said, let's discuss how to prevent an offset so we don't get into that *very long* minefield of red tape.

Consolidation

Assuming you don't qualify for forgiveness, the Direct Loan program can be your ticket out of this mess - if you're not too deep in the hole. One option is to group your loans together which would take your loan out of default and put it in good standing. The other is IBR, or Income Based Repayment. If you're making pennies working at 7-Eleven then you'll likely pay nothing. Nada. Zero. But the time to get approved can take one to three months. You can do the math at the link below:

http://www.ibrinfo.org/calculator.php

The other thing to remember about consolidation is that your interest rate must factor into any decisions you make. My advice is to wait until you are out of school before accruing additional loans by consolidation - when the interest rate is locked at a low amount.

Rehabilitation

Many students apply for rehabilitating their loans, which takes nine months. Talk with your lender to work out a payment plan. When the rehab process is complete, default status is changed to good standing. At issue is this: students are eligible for taking out massive student loans (again!) which does not help the situation.

Forbearance: This should be the last bullet in your holster. If all of the above fails, you can put your loan into forbearance. This helps stave off the vampiric collectors but with a terrible price: excessive interest! We're talking biblical revelatory interest here, called capitalized interest that will kill any business before it gets off the ground. Then there are fees the lender likes to tack on. Debt slavery is alive and well.

Those are the legal ways to deal with student loans.

The shady way is to just let them default. If you go this route, they will call and harass you dozens of times per day. They will hound your relatives and friends and colleagues. It will show up on a credit report for a potential employer to see. And that's not even the most absurd part. Want to know what is?

Okay, here it is: They're not really interested in you paying them back. They're interested in you putting them back into deferral/forbearance so they can charge you insane *interest* - which they fleece the taxpayers to pay.

Bottom line: Pay something. Anything. Even fifty dollars a month. Heck even ten dollars a month by money order is something traceable you can show a judge, heaven forbid it should ever come to that.

Social Security Numbers

If you've ever spent time googling your own name, you know how easy it is to find *other people* with the same name as you. I googled my own and found a pepper-bearded lawyer in Tennessee with the exact same name that I have using peoplelookup.com

The guy was the same age, had the same name, but looked differently. I write for a living. He sues people for a living.

But... we have different social security numbers. He probably uses his for just about everything under the sun, including applying for work before he went lawyering up. I don't. Reason being is that I don't like where I sleep and fart being known by every red-headed harpy named Betty who works in HR. So to that I've used a fake address for as long as I remember. When I don't have the luxury of using my own, I used a friend's address. As any privacy-minded man should.

Employment

Back in 2008 when Obama took office and the economy nose-dived, I applied in person to some 600 jobs to supplement my income. I must have lost a hundred pounds hitting the pavement. The overwhelming response in 98% of the jobs I applied for?

Apply online.

It mattered not what establishment I went to. FedEx. Home Depot. Publishers. Newspapers. They all said the same thing: Apply online. Apply online. Apply online. I heard those two words so much that I began to see them in my digital alarm clock, blinking like some countdown on a thermonuclear device. Worse was the fact that many asked me for my social security number *before* being hired. I found it all appalling and disrespectful of someone's privacy.

Never, ever give this out before you're hired. Doing so will set you in the crosshairs of any collectors or private eyes out there looking to gun you down. The two jobs I did secure hired me because I'd given an obvious fake social number prior to hiring (1234-56-7890). The interviewer, a man, could have cared less though I did fork over my real one when they said, "Welcome aboard."

Things to Avoid

Universities

When I attended the University of New Orleans, the social security number was used for nearly everything. Checking out books. Scheduling classes. Asking for grade transcripts. I worked in the Financial Aid office and there, too, I found few students were referred to by name. You were just a number. I would call up to schedule an appointment and the first thing they'd say, before anything else:

"What's your social?"

Pathetic.

Even more pathetic was that anyone who worked in the UNO system had access to this number. It mattered not how secure the system was against identity theft because any schmuck who'd just transferred in could work in any department he wanted as long as the work-study money was there. Free money, they called it.

Taxpayer money. Be careful about throwing this number around like monopoly money.

Class Rosters

This was another biggie.

On my way to the restroom, I happened to notice one professor had every student's SSN beside their name on the class roster. I began to wonder why this was, and if other professors did the same for all other classes. Sadly, there wasn't anything I could really do about it at the time.

Computer Labs

Back when we had a VAX system at UNO, around the time Netscape became popular, we had to use our SSN to login. This same login scheme was how one Harvard student was busted in 2014 when he used Tor to send a bomb threat... out of sheer boredom! Not too bright.

The other threat is that students walking by you in a lab setting can see you type it out. Heck they can even see you from behind since in many labs the chairs are fitted close together to accommodate a sea of new students every semester. Avoid this if you can by logging in from your own laptop.

Grades Listed Outside Class

I was a pre-med gunner before switching to computer science. In my freshman chemistry class, grades were posted outside the classroom in the hall, listed with everyone else's social security number. I watched in disbelief as many a student slid his finger down the list to see his grade. If I were the nefarious type, it would have been a no-brainer to match the kid with the social number and execute the beginnings of a clever identity theft scheme.

I scratched mine out with a Sharpie marker.

Dorms

My first semester of college had me and my brother lugging my few meager possessions up six floors of my dormitory. But prior to that, I had to check in. But checking in was done *outdoors*, just outside the entryway.

I had to present my driver's license to show I wasn't some old Cajun bum dropout from culinary school to shack up with the girls going to and fro. They checked my name on a paper roster to see which room I had been assigned. I requested a single one. They laughed. And there next to my name was my social security number. Wonderful, I thought. That number again.

There have been a few incidents with social security numbers being stolen over the years and used for all kinds of mischief overseas. Now you may be thinking, why would someone go to all that trouble? Steal someone else's social security number so they can do... what exactly?

Well, I'll tell you. If you're a criminal, the best thing in the world is to steal someone else's identity. For this reason, you should never, ever use someone else's number. That other person can be on the FBI's Most Wanted list and the day you find that out will be too late without them charging you with identity theft *yourself*.

Changing Your Name Stateside

Changing your name isn't difficult. It's getting a new SSN that's a pain in the patella. It isn't like reaching into a bag of Skittles. More often than not, it's done by a court order. The requirements are beyond strict, placing the burden of proof on you, the ever law-abiding citizen, one being that you must prove to a court of law that you are in danger of losing your life. And you need to *prove* it, not just say it. This might be an abusive spouse who tried to kill you or the FBI's Witness Protection Plan or some such, but the social security number will likely stay with you without this.

Here is what the government says about getting a new number (at the ssa.gov site):

We do not routinely assign different Social Security numbers. Generally, only the following circumstances are used to assign a different number:

Sequential numbers have been assigned to members of the same family and are causing problems; More than one person has been assigned, or is using, the same number;

An individual has religious or cultural objections to certain numbers or digits in the original number;

A victim of identity theft continues to be disadvantaged by using the original number; or

Situations of harassment, abuse, or life endangerment, including domestic violence, has occurred.

White Lies

Privacy advocates, no matter how careful, cannot get around the social security number requirements on FAFSA (financial aid) forms without risking them saying no. If you use a fake SSN, you can be charged with a felony. So what to do?

What you do is lie to *everyone else*. For instance:

There was a time when I was contacted by a collection agency. TransMediaCorp or some innocuous name. Usually when a collection agency calls, if you listen closely you can hear all the other script monkeys banging away on their keyboards in the background, chatting away (mostly lies). My answer was to lie right back to them.

"Is this Mr. X?" agent Betty asked.

"Mr. Who?" I shot back. (Always, always get them to repeat it!)

She repeated. I feigned deafness. "Say it once more?"

She did, and at that point I corrected her, saying she had the right first name but the wrong *last name.* It was misspelled and mispronounced. I feigned being insulted.

They had the wrong guy. Tough break. She then asked for my social security number. I gave her a false one for the simple reason that as soon as you identify yourself (it is, after all, the first question they'll ask), you paint a blood-red target on your back. They've matched the name with a legal address. From then on it'll be one perpetual nightmare after another.

The amount in question was a $500 Perkins student loan I'd paid off years earlier, and one that I'd taken on some 25 years ago. But I wasn't about to tell *her* that. God knows if I did, they might consider the debt paid after I faxed proof of payment, but not before they relayed my name to other collection agencies for *their* databases.

After this episode, I called up every service provider I could think of that held my social security number and had it changed to the fictitious one. Cable company. Electric. Internet Service Provider. It turned out that even the company that mows my lawn had it on file. Who knows how they got it, but one company gave me grief over the change: the power company. So, I handled it in writing, making sure to use plenty of CAPS and BOLD words filled with sound and fury (signifying nothing, now that I think about it).

Some people can better sense a bluff over the phone than in the mail. By mail, you can sound like Tony Soprano and if you don't get some action you will send the boys over for a *polite little talk*.

Clone Home

One option you might employ is using a mail service that severs any connection to you. Examples abound of companies you can hire who ask very few questions. A few ask *zero* questions. I've had good experience with earthclassmail.com, for instance, but there are others if you travel internationally.

Another idea is to check out abandoned houses where you live. Mostly this applies to city dwellers but I have found a few in rural settings, too. Use the address of the abandoned house to have any shipments or mail sent to you there. Just don't go using the same house over and over again.

It's probably is a good time to repeat this: Never give out someone else's information on a credit card or loan application. Like, ever. This includes their address. In most first world countries this is a serious crime. Someone somewhere will get burned as one success will lead to another and it will become a habit that is as hard to get rid of as an alcoholic getting rid of margaritas in Maui. It can also destroy any chance you have if, at a later date, you want to legally get rid of debt via bankruptcy.

Lie, but lie responsibly!

Passports and Canada

This is an area I regret having personal experience in. Since 9/11, many systems have been built for interdepartmental communications, yet airports *still* have lax security. Especially the TSA.

Border Stations are an interesting study and I dare say Canadian Border Officers are, fortunately, nothing like their lackluster TSA brethren down south. Only what gets flagged at one Canadian station gets flagged at them all. It's a little too Orwellian for my liking, but I try to be respectful whenever I'm passing through. If I didn't? Well, there's problems.

If you drop attitude with the Canadian agent at the Niagara Falls crossing, the guard on the other side of the country can know about it (notice I didn't say *will*) in minutes if he enters it into the system.

The social security system is tied to your name and employment, but does not appear on the passport itself. But a border official *can* ban you for life if you lie about any criminal record entering Canada. They locked out George Bush from entering over a DUI he'd received in 1976. No kidding. He had to get a waiver and that was just to *visit*, not actually move there.

Sneaking in carries risks too, unless you happen to be Nightcrawler from the X-Men and can teleport yourself in the blink of an eye across the Falls. As far as I know, I don't possess this ability.

But I have learned a valuable lesson: Do not leave trails.

One option is to not use our passport since it leaves a trail. But this is not very practical since without it you cannot travel internationally. Still, sneaking into Canada or into the United States does have its advantages if you have good reason to go off the grid. Many do. In fact, the U.S. border sees more sneak *into* Canada than the other way.

This is from the WinnipegPress:

"More people were caught trying to sneak into Canada at remote border points with the United States in 2008 than the other way around, a newly released intelligence report reveals.

It was the second straight year that continental human smuggling and other surreptitious crossings tilted in Canada's direction.

*The RCMP attributes the trend to factors including a U.S. crackdown on undocumented workers, more American agents along the border and the shaky state of the U.S. economy. The figures, the latest available, show 952 people were caught entering Canada between legitimate border crossings, while 819 were U.S.-bound. They work at strategic points between border crossings to thwart smugglers of everything from **people** and **drugs** to **currency** and **firearms**."*

Obviously, sneaking across is not a new trend. But let's assume you need to sneak into Canada and need to do it quietly, with no Orwellian tracking system sniffing at your heels. Let's also assume you're going to do it solo. Zero assistance.

Without Assistance

Crossing outside a checkpoint is very easy. Nothing to it in fact. But doing it anonymously, now that's *hard*. Harder in big towns. It's illegal to try and you might not get caught the first time. But most guys will keep doing what they think works the best and then rinse and repeat. If they succeed on the first try, well dag nabbit, they're ingenious! Rinse and repeat.

Bank robbers usually don't get caught the first time either. It's when they do it again and again using the same method that gets them caught. Their egos rocket into orbit. They get overconfident. They get cocky. In fact you could apply this trait to most low-level crimes, even non-violent ones like sneaking across.

The border itself looks like a typical power line cut, forests on each side but the further you get from a town, the less guarded it is. But you should know the ecosystem of whatever area regardless if you plan to hike or drive or fly through because, let's face it, it'd be quite a downer to make all that effort only to be the next contestant on Mr. Grizzly's 'You Bet Your Life'.

Most rural spots and undeveloped areas are heavily guarded by movement sensors. Trigger one of those and you'll alert the authorities.

Response time vary significantly, depending on population and distance to the nearest checkpoint and of course, manpower. All the technology in the world does the Borg no good at all if the Borg drones are overworked and stretched to the limit. This is in your favor.

It may be an hour or ten minutes before one arrives. If the latter, you'll walk a little ways before the border patrol drives up. But, after you get to meet Officer Simon Sez who carries a semi-automatic rifle along with four of his buddies, one of whom will ask you point blank: "Do you realize where you are, sir?" To which you should state with an innocent smile as you look around, feigning relief that you happened upon this nice Canadian officer: "Hale no sir, I don't believe I do. Can you please tell us?"

Politeness with a dash of respect (*always* saying sir) will win over a Canadian border guard 80% of the time, assuming you're not committing a crime, and you are if you're sneaking across!

But that's if you get lucky. If not, you'll be arrested and deported if you don't have dual-citizenship. Not only will Canadian authorities charge and fine you, so will American authorities. It's a $5000 US fine and criminal record for circumventing a designated border crossing.

With Assistance

Very much the easier of the two since it's not exactly rocket science to get you across the border in either a privately owned plane or smaller-than-usual boat or other watercraft. Better still if you're smuggled in close to a Mohawk native reservation where cigarette smugglers get picked up all the time (and overlooked) by Canadian border officials.

In the event you do try to cross, make sure it's not the 'easy path' others take. It's all an illusion setup by the RCMP to catch you on a well-worn trail. Most people caught do something stupid like crossing at the Silver Lake Road area or farm land close to the Huntingdon/Sumas crossing. Every time I hear of a bust, and the details that come from that bust, I think of what the T-Rex hunter Roland said in Jurassic Park: Lost World, when he tells Hammond's successor to forget about setting base camp at their present location - a location that's plagued with velociraptors.

"Listen, we're on a game trail and carnivores *hunt* on game trails! Do you want to setup base camp or a buffet?"

Smuggling anything like contraband by way of car is foolish. There are sensors at border crossings. Those include vehicle scanning x-ray machines, chemical sniffers and sniffer dogs. So any attempt to hide in a vehicle heading into Canada just won't work either. The GlobeandMail ironically enough (in an article titled: How Smugglers Miss the Hidden Eyes) went into further detail on what not to do, even revealing that some hotels along the border are under surveillance for illegal crossers.

Bottom line: Don't ever go into velociraptor territory on the cheap!

Anonymous Phones - How the FBI Traces Calls

Not every average Joe who loathes the NSA has something illegal to hide, and I'm about as average Joe as you can get. I enjoy shrimp at Red Lobster. I love Mardi Gras in the French Quarter whenever I visit. I play video games with the kids down at the Fun Arcade. And sometimes while they play, I conduct business on prepaid phones called *burners*. Burners the NSA doesn't like. In fact, they have a real hard time linking those phones to my real identity. It isn't impossible, mind you, only difficult. Since I am not a high-value target, they don't bother.

At least, I *hope* they don't bother.

Now then, you probably already know about MVNOs (Mobile Virtual Network Operators) that allow you to sign up pseudo-anonymously. They ask for no identifying info unless you want to give it to them - but that alone is not enough to thwart the NSA. Phone companies are now required to have the technology to work with law enforcement under the 1994 CALEA law.

Worse still is the fact that despite what appeals courts have said, we still have no real expectation of privacy. Most state laws dictate that as long as one person knows about the recording, it's legal. Note I did not say one other person. Only one person, the one doing the recording. Wiretap laws are a maze of red tape that would make Stalin blush. The counter is this: not everyone uses the same phone. That's in our favor.

Can you imagine the power a federal government might wield if *everyone* in the nation used the same PC setup? Right, I thought so.

Moving on...

The Cons of Using a Burner

You can pitch it in the trash after its used and dissolve any trail to you. That's it, as long as you took action to conceal your activity. The Craigslist killer was caught by the FBI by cell triangulation; the GPS signals from his real phone and prepaid phone came from the same place. He even had it on him when he bought the burner phone. When he killed someone, both phones were easily traced since he had them on him when he committed the crime. Not so smart, but then most criminals don't get caught the first or second time. They get caught on the *third, fourth* or *fifth* time. Remember bank robbers? The adrenaline rush addicts them to the point they're always looking for the next fix, often without upgrading their skill set.

The MAC address can kill anonymity as well. Like the IP address for computers tied to a network, it can lead right to your front door. There are apps like Macspoofer that aid in preventing this, but they are not perfect.

The Pros of Using a Burner Phone

Number one rule: Do not use it continually for any sensitive business or personal transactions. No more than a few days for something important. If you're on vacation in say in Singapore, and don't want the NSA spying on you and the kids, that's easy. Just switch the SIM cards out on arrival. Same for Philippines, Thailand, etc.

But for something like spying, well that's a whole other discussion. One might say, "Well, if I'm running a North Korean spy op, why not bypass any surveillance by having my entire team switch to newly bought phones at the same time?"

The problem with that is, then you've created a clear pattern of a group of phones all activating at the same time. You might even get careless and give each operative the same phones. Further, if the police obtain the IMEI code from the burner, then all SIM links previously attached to the phones are discovered. Good for them. Not for you.

You could even be outwitted if they visit the places they *think* you will buy the prepaid burners - obtain the IMEI numbers in advance so as to get a search warrant to eavesdrop on you. Boom. And you have to know that not all team members will dispose of the phones after every communiqué. Problems, problems. So what to do?

Solution:

- Manage two persons responsible for managing all phones.

- Buy phones from different locations, different days, different purchasers.
- Swap phones out at different intervals from random locations (cell towers).
- Issue to operatives at different dates.
- Operatives don't know when phones were activated.
- Retire some phones unexpectedly, some sooner, after risky operations for example.
- Each Operative is given set of other Operative's numbers, which change daily.

The above is admittedly overkill for the average Joe of course, but this should give you an idea of what's required to evade NSA tracking, as well as the local cops. In ten years we may end up reverting back to this...

Disappearing from Social Media

Let's cut right to the chase. Social Media did nothing for me but make disappearing harder. With every passing year, Facebook wanted more data on me. More of my favorite childhood cereals (Chocolate Frosted Sugar Bombs, I told them - the favorite of Calvin and Hobbes). More of which movies made me cry. Which made me angry. Which made me cringe (the skeleton reveal in Psycho).

Employers love this about social media. They love that they can google your name and find all kinds of dirt on you from Ars Technica posts to Usenet flame wars you've participated in over the years.

Once upon a time, Usenet was sacred. You didn't talk about Usenet. Now it's monitored by Chinese law enforcement. Yet things I wrote ten years back are visible to anyone. My inner child mutant came storming out, fists clenched, teeth gritted and spitting insults before the troll meme became fashionable.

While we can't exactly take a Delorean back to 1985 and start nuking old newsgroup posts, what you can do is take a flamethrower to the media giants who aren't doing your career any favors by allowing your ex to post photos of you so drunk in the French Quarter that you performed mouth to mouth on a fainted carriage mule... who you could swear winked at you as it went down.

Phase 1: Nuking the Sites From Orbit

I nuked my own Facebook account in May of 2010. Little did I know, however, that it wasn't truly gone. Instead, it went into a kind of hibernation state. Surprise, surprise. Facebook, like Google and LinkedIn and Twitter and YouTube all have this egregious habit of what I call vampire hoodwinking. They lull you into thinking your account is gone which it really isn't. Nothing is really permanently gone with any of those behemoths. Not Google, Facebook or even LinkedIn. It would take the fires of Mt. Doom to do to your account what it did to Frodo's ring.

But let's try anyway.

Facebook

Use this link to delete your account.

https://www.facebook.com/help/delete_account

This isn't like tossing out a batch of brownies when you're on a new diet. This effect is supposedly permanent. You're not going to get it back. You can't salvage anything for a new account. So contact lists, favorites, bookmarks, posts, pictures... all gone unless you saved them locally to your hard drive or Dropbox. Now might be a good time to ask for some awkward pics to be taken down.

Twitter

As well, now might be a good time to deactivate your Twitter account. Like Facebook, once it's gone, it's GONE. But the process takes time. When I deleted one of my pen names, a horror pen that wasn't selling, it took *seven* days and a full moon. I never was good at writing omens.

Google+

For Google, go to the homepage at accounts.google.com to deactivate. This will nuke your Gmail and Youtube accounts as well, since they tie everything together. But you can be more selective at plus.google.com in what you wish to leave. They call it "Downgrading," but you should know that your identity might still pop up in search engines. Sucks, doesn't it?

I've found <u>AccountKiller</u> to be of high value here, as there were some accounts still active that I hadn't used in years, but a few that had stored my present phone number and address **publicly**. Enhancements, they claimed.

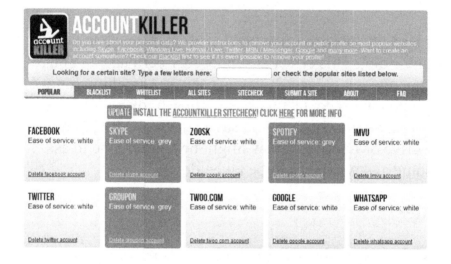

Phase 2: Nuking Criminal and Public Records

Now we come to the area where Skip Tracers love to dig, and dig DEEP. We're talking Gimli's drunken dwarf king deep who loves to delve in places he shouldn't (how'd that turn out for him?).

Without any background information, they will be chasing ghosts and wild geese to who knows where. Bad for them. Good for us. We'll nuke what remnants of our social selves are ripe for the taking - which in the end only hurts *us*, after all. As we go through these, realize this is a very short list and if there is one thing I love about Reddit, it's that they don't believe in short lists.

There is a short version, that is, the major players:

Spokeo - This is the big one. The one every Skip Tracer and collector uses by default. The amount of data they had on me made me want to retch my In n' Out burger! Former email addresses. Relationships. Marriages. Schools. For a few dollars more they'd probably go tell a collector if I put ketchup on my fries or on the side. The kind of guys Agent Smith might call up to find out where Neo was hiding in The Matrix.

Intelius - I was in this database too, but not for any criminal activity (whew!). Like Spokeo, they keep a lot of data on people without asking first. Not Agent Smith's first choice, but if Spokeo is down... it is. They trawl social media sites as well as keep criminal data. Rumor has it mugshots are on the way. Are Christmas morning pictures next?

Zabasearch - I used this one once to find an old phone number I'd forgotten and didn't want to call up every friend to relay the new one. Later I found that this is THE site to use if you're a stalker since, after June 2014, emails containing personal info (not searchable by search engines) became publicly available. Ouch.

Going through every site that I'd given my data to over the last ten years was like trying to defect from a vampire clan. Easier said than done. They want something signed in blood. The worst, however, is hitting *paywalls* and *upsells*. You know, people who claim to save you *money* and *time*.

One site did seem to help shorten time taken to erase myself from the internet. That site is DeleteMe, at abine.com, and at $129 bucks, it ain't cheap. But if you're strapped for time and don't mind the fee then it can be worth your while.

Staying Off The Radar

For the next two years you must be consistent with updates. Check those sites every few months for your compliance. Google your name. Your old phone numbers. Old addresses. Old flames. Your identity after all is more valuable to you than it is to them. To them, you're simply a number in a database, and if they had their way, wouldn't mind too terribly the thought of tattooing a number on the back of your neck.

From the moment of Armageddon, I've used Fake Name Generator for many things I do online. You can too. Yes, it does sound like some two-bit app on the Google Play Store that Babu wrote in Bombay one summer's day, but I assure you it isn't. It's quite effective.

If you want free, DISPOSABLE mail, try Mailinator (no relation to Arnold). No signup required. No passwords.

Stalkers

For some reason stalkers tend to be overwhelmingly male when Hollywood spits them out. I can count the number of female stalker flicks on one hand: Fatal Attraction. Misery. The Crush. Those're the ones I've seen. And they make the male ones look pale by comparison. Stick the knife into poor Jimmy and laugh in his face.

That's not exactly realistic though, since they're always a thousand times worse on the silver screen than up close. Most stalkers are your next-door neighbor types. But sometimes, well... sometimes there's an exception. An anomaly if you will that slices to bits any preconceived notion of what a stalker looks and acts like. They break all the rules.

What follows is my own story. It's one memory I can't quite seem to delete from my memory banks no matter how hard I try. And lordy, who knows why. Perhaps it's the dark elements of the unknown. What *could* have happened. What she could have done had I not taken it as seriously as I did. Even now my fingers hurt from the constant flexing, cracked-knuckle strain I exert as I contemplate the telling of it all.

But I'll leave out the truly disgusting parts in case you're just having lunch.

The Bayou Grandma Stalker

The new house I'd rented was as good as any, I'd guessed. Way out there too, out near the bayou and close to La Place and *juuust* outside Kenner, Louisiana but far enough from the traffic and airport that it squashed any worries about jet engines flying overhead.

But the mosquitoes, sweet Jesus were they BIG. Winged vampires with probos so darn big you'd swear you'd been shot in the butt with a poison dart like one of them pigmy tribes make.

My father had rented the place to parolees - mostly thieves from what I'd heard. Big time, small time, bank robbers, shoplifters, pimps. Didn't matter what kind. It'd been far enough out of town so as to limit temptation, he'd said, but a couple months passed with no takers. Enter yours truly on a 3-month dry spell in book sales and just generally unemployable for eons.

I still remember his words as he handed me the key: "Don't turn the place into a dirty whorehouse. Sheriff don't like that."

"Whore? What're those?" I asked. He smiled back. That toothless grin of his never put me at ease like it did when I was five, but now I knew how much of a hard-ass he was.

I only paid a quarter rent in exchange for repairing the place, but lordy how I loathed crawling under the house to fix *anything*. It wasn't the tarantulas I feared. It was that dadgum Daddy-long-leg spiders that spooked me the most. Mobs! I'd bang out 1000 new words daily (my self-imposed quota at the time) and they'd bang out 10000 baby spiders as I typed the last word. On some dark nights I could swear I heard em popping out under the floorboards like popcorn in a microwave.

Pop-pop-pop-pop-pop-pop.

Then things got louder in July. Peeper frogs amid every god-forsaken bog noise in the universe kept me up. You'd think I'd have gotten use to em, but no. Afternoons were only slightly better. I made a promise to keep busy. I'd survey the property, check mail, repair pipes, try not to sweat too much as it killed my writing mood, when one day I noticed something off.

Some of my mail looked opened. In fact it looked *read*. That feeling, you know? Smudges. Strange scents. Like the kind church ladies wear on Sunday. Letters were out of order, too. Bills were upside down like someone'd repacked them after sticking a cherry bomb into the mailbox.

Humidity, maybe.

I walked down the lonely road to meet the neighbor I'd put off meeting. A neighbor who lived in a house that *leaned* toward the airport, like the wood wanted to fly off and forever be rid of this frog-infested mudhole. Spooky branches prevented this, of course. "You're staying here," the wood seemed to say.

Anyway I knocked and knocked. No answer. Went around back, knocked some more, ridged my forehead and looked around as I wiped away sweat and scratched. The bog seemed far quieter here despite La Place more than living up to its reputation as the Saharan desert of marshes.

I left a note, an invitation for the neighbor to come by and share a beer with me, the new guy (or an iced tea and a Bigfoot flick, if a lady). A guy could hope, right?

After heading home I banged out 1500 more words and popped in The Thing as I kicked back a couple of Buds. "Where's Blair?" a voice said into the gloom. Ah, I'd forgotten the electricity had cut out midway the previous Saturday. I ignored the creaky boards under my feet and sank into the couch. Dusty as hell, it was like sinking into a puffy mushroom. The kind some British kids like to play soccer with.

Just when the movie got to the gross "Let's see who's The Thing" blood-test-by-self-inflicted-razor, I heard a noise. I sat up just as, once again, the electricity shut off.

Shit. Then, a catty sound. Mauling. Yawning slow kind of sound. What the hell?

......scratch....scratch....scraaaaatch.

The door, I thought. I crept to the door over-thinking it as usual. A cat? Not a chance - too slow to be a cat. This was more like a *taunt*. A set of nails being dragged across a chalkboard to grate someone's nerves kind of taunt. *My* nerves.

I looked out the window. Darkness looked back at me. I started flexing my fingers and cracking my knuckle one-handedly. Think rational. Think logically. But the darkness was so thick it seemed stitched into the clothing of whomever had disturbed me. Intense camouflage. *Whoever* it was, was standing out there. I could swear I saw *something*. Something frozen so stiff and absolute it was as though dark matter had enveloped it. Despite this, I hated the thought of showing fear by running to get my revolver in the bedroom. No, I thought, and frowned chewing on my bottom lip. I'd face this punky prankster head on.

I swung the screen door open so hard it flew off the hinges.

The monolithic figure was gone. Not a soul stood there, nothing at all but boggy air. I stepped out and as I did waved the fog away. Nothing, absolutely nothing, made a sound. Not even peeper frogs.

A few days later I walked next door once more, determined as ever to find out if my neighbor knew of any rascally kids making mischief in these mossy parts. God knew they had nothing better to do.

This time I met her: a sweet old lady that could never harm a fly. She invited me in. She even made tea and biscuits. A British lady with a midnight cat straight out of Sleepy Hollow. Herself? Liverpool from the sound of it. Who knew but what I did know was that she had a class and a grace I couldn't quite match due to my swampbilly upbringing. I let her prattle on and simply nodded and hmm'ed and smiled rather than allow my lips to leak my ignorance.

French-Acadian lineages was the topic, her *spessscialty,* apparently. Not my cup of tea, but I listened anyway as she did most of the talking and I just sat there like a bump on a log soaking it all in. And that she did with a vengeance! Talked my ear clean off as frogs croaked outside.

Ten minutes into it, my mind wandered and I noticed a faint lisp. I stared at her wrinkled lips as they quivered and bounced from topic to topic and saw an oddity. No, not her lips. Her *tongue.* Her tongue looked cut. A small one to be sure, right at the tip that affected her speech. Was I seeing things? The day was hot and hazy.

A paper cut? I wondered.

The only time I'd ever done that myself was when I licked an envelope a little too fast.

Lightning struck.

She'd half-assed the licking of my envelopes somehow. When this light bulb bloomed in my head, I noticed her eyes widen and her speech crawl. I coulda sworn I heard her heart speed up as a dark narrative began to unroll in my thoughts. She knew I knew. She had to! It was written right there in her liquid-green eyes.

I excused myself to the restroom and on the way back cut through the kitchen and out of the corner of my eye saw a familiar name next to a Home Sweet Home frame with a few scattered nails. It was an open envelope with my name on it.

I gritted my teeth so hard my loose tooth almost popped out. That crinkly old thief!

I paused to rub my chin, my neck, both my eyes. Maybe I was just imagining things, I told myself. Working too hard. Worrying too much. Swamp fever perhaps, or maybe the mailman simply slipped one into the wrong box. I'd done that myself a few times working campus mail back in the day.

But I just couldn't stomach the thought of that old bat, smart as she was, scraping through my mail. Scraping *my* things. Stabbing *my* privacy in the back. Stalking me. And for what reason? So I called her on it in as polite a way as I could fathom yet fully expecting a sincere apology, to which I'd apologize right back.

I was wrong.

Her face *changed* right before my eyes. I thought I was hallucinating at first. That maybe the old witch had poisoned my tea with some dart frog resin. Those sweet, elderly church fingers clenched as she stared at the floor coldly, the paleness of her jaw becoming steely, a kind of veil of jaundice sliding over her face. She seemed to be turning to stone!

It was a look I had never seen even in a hardened criminal. A faraway, ancient look, like she'd just celebrated her 2000th birthday and here I was spoiling her party by not outstretching my own wrists. And when she fixed her cataract eyes on me, I nearly bolted for the door right then and there. She noticed this and said,

"Well now, dearie. It seems that you've c--"

Before she could finish, I tipped my old Port Authority cap and exited before she could finish. That was it. I was out of there, permanently.

Later when I asked my father to look into her past, it turned out she was anything but the nice, country granny I'd believed. She'd done time for murder, theft and chronic shoplifting. Oh, and slapping a judge as he sat in Preservation Hall just inside the French Quarter. Just walked right up to him. Brilliant. This on top of the sweet, sugar-coated lies she told me, smiling like a Cheshire cat right into my face.

I was forced to move three days later due to further circus-monkey antics.

The old crone stole my mail as though each and every one of them were sealed with liquid gold.

But there was more. She broke into my house while I vacationed way up in Thunder Bay, Ontario. I'd set up a hidden cam to silence my naysaying father, hoping to catch her in the act and send her to the Big House once again with all the other harpies. Only I failed.

She'd spent hours simply rocking back and forth in my living room with her black cat (who kindly relieved himself behind my couch). My father laughed. Pointed, and laughed. But I was determined. I did some more digging.

It turned out she had a son that died a year prior running from police after a robbery. A son with a history of crime with a face *remarkably* like mine. I could sense some residue of reason behind her madness.

Only now I cannot watch John Carpenter's The Thing without smelling that darn cat.

~ ~ ~

So then, what did I learn from this? What can *you* learn?

I learned that stalkers come in all sizes and flavors of the rainbow and, in all likelihood, will never be a stranger to you. You'll know this person personally. They may even be in a relationship with you. Celebrities have the cash to deal with them: Catherine Zeta-Hones and Dave Letterman come to mind. Guys like you and me must use our wits since we're not winning the lottery anytime soon.

Willy Wonka's Stalker Factory

These are just some of the different types of stalkers I've met over the years. They remind me of the kids from Willy Wonka and the Chocolate Factory. Some of them are as sweet as Valentine candy. Others, well...

The Rejected Partner: We've all seen this kind. They feel they'd been slighted and want to settle the score since the other person got the upper hand, the last laugh.

The Bluffer Stalker: These are the guys who are mostly bark but no bite. They bluff frequently, issuing threats and grievances, but rarely take it as far as physical violence. A few might call in a bomb threat when there is no bomb. The judge usually gives them a few years to think it over.

The Celebrity Stalker: These tend to break into celebrity houses, thinking that if they just force a confrontation with ol' Dave, he just might share his wealth and invite them to live in his humble, little abode and make great comedy sketches with them every night before the announcer says, "It's the Late Show with Daaaaaavid Letterrrrman!"

Not happening.

True Predators: The dangerous ones. The child kidnappers. The dottering, old crones who just might be pushed over the edge to "adopt" a son that looks suspiciously like the one they'd lost a year prior, even if that means embalming him. They may have only known the victim for a little while as well.

Validation

Stalkers loathe the absence of constant validation. They need it. You provide it. The solution is not to provide it since they feed off of it like vampires (sensing a trend, here?) and the kicker is that they feel you love them simply because of that first encounter, an encounter that was run-of-the-mill for *you* but equivalent to meeting the Messiah for *them*.

They leave notes. They call you constantly. They become a thorn in your side. The more details you give them, that's another spark plug for the emotion engine, an engine fueled by your own niceness. So you must be firm and vigilant and above all else, be capable to laying down your law.

The Hitchhiker

In the 1990s, I picked up a hitchhiker on my way from New Orleans to a local Mississippi college to inquire about teaching for a semester. It was a long ride. My radio was broken. I could use some nice conversation, I thought. Besides that, he looked like a clean-cut, Leave-It-To-Beaver type. You've seen them: Sharp dresser. Smooth talker. Great big smile with a perfect row of teeth. The perfect guy to sell a Porsche to someone with eight of them already. The kind of guy you'd trust with your own daughter in your weekend cabin for the weekend but who'd later break her heart in half, lickety-split. When he got into the car, he smelled like Georgio cologne and cigarettes.

Well we got to talking about everything under the sun. Politics. The weather. The cool new age music on the Weather Channel that he wanted so badly to identify. Pat Metheny, I'd said.

We even talked about Mississippi girls compared to Canadian girls. A world of difference, actually. I asked him what he was studying. His reply?

"I want to be a sorcerer just like my daddy."

I nearly hit a fire hydrant just as a dog was doing his business. By god, I had a male wiccan in my car dressed like Bill Gates.

Before I could laugh at this obvious joke he was playing on me, he proceeded to lay out his whole philosophy of life, real slow and methodical like, waving his fingers around like a magician.

I began to ask him questions about this so-called "career." As it turned out, I had to give him personal information about me for every question I asked. Sort of like bartering for dummies. A power thing to him, obviously. Personal validation was everything, *as was his image*. I went along with it just as my hands became sweat-filled on the steering wheel and by the time I dropped him off at his destination, I said a little prayer of thanks to the Almighty that the guy never pulled a gun on me.

Would he have? I don't know. Maybe. Maybe not.

Bottom line? Appearances are deceptive. That includes: Scents. Visuals. Touch. Audio. Strangers can get into your head and stay there unless you say one word at the outset:

"NO."

Say no to clinginess and control-freaks who'd rather you hang out with them then visit your dying mother in the retirement home.

Now, I was beyond polite with him. A lot of guys I know in Mississippi wouldn't. They'd boot his butt right out as soon as he prattled on about his plans to conquer the world with "Dark Energy."

But if you do *that*, you're gonna risk trouble. Be firm, but polite. Don't say, "Get the hell outta my truck, Bozo!" Say,

"That's interesting," which I did. To which he replied, "So do you accept my philosophy, brother?"

He called me brother the entire trip and it always coincided with him touching my knee.

I feigned ignorance, explaining I needed him to tell me more. More. More. More... all the way to the college. It worked. But he did demand my phone number and address at the end. Fake, of course.

Violence ensues if you take the wrong road, and that certainly might have happened if I'd brought his whole self-image crumbling to the ground. Leave the "tough-love" talk for someone else. A judge, maybe.

Ruin Her Life! (Tell the World)

If the stalker comes back for more trolling mischief, tell everyone you know about it. I mean *everyone*. One post on a blog might even do it if they're all reading. There's something to be said for safety in numbers, and when all eyes are on him, or her, and they know you've told your family, friends and even the police, they'll likely back off since most crave solitude more than the spotlight.

The other thing is this: Never consider a stalker's comments harmless. One of my favorite authors on this subject, John Moore, Ph.D, who has done a ton of stuff for WebMD, put it best with his description of the "Obsessive Love Wheel", that circle of pattern that almost all controlling ex-lovers, friends or family exhibit:

1.) The Attraction Phase

2.) The Anxiety Phase, where warning signs start to appear.

3.) Obsessive - The stalker ramps up the threats.

4.) Violence Phase - Where you can literally disappear one day, since the stalker at this point knows your schedules, and thus every move you make.

Securing Your Computer

When I relayed to my grandmother last Christmas that I write books on anonymity and how to become invisible, she nearly gagged on her macadamia nut cookie. I got dead air. I thought maybe I'd given her a heart attack. Then came the lecture. I was going to get arrested by the FBI and every other alphabet agency. I'd be waterboarded. Chipped. Brainwashed. I'd be the next Edward Snowden (though I'm not nearly as handsome).

People, old people especially, tend to group the word anonymity under a pretty big umbrella that includes hackers, spies and contract killers. If you've got an encrypted hard drive, then you've got something to hide, perhaps the location to where you buried Jimmy Hoffa.

"Encryption?" she asked, "I hope you're not hanging around one of those Goodfella guys. Besides, isn't that illegal, dearie? Hm?"

"Not on your life, and thank heavens for small miracles. But I can tell you this: " I reassured, "Even if I were, I'd *still* teach people how to secure their own data somehow. Keep it away from snoops."

"But we're all snoops, dear."

"True, but some are more snoopy than others."

"But dearest, I don't want you getting into trouble with the government. They're our friend y'know and they know best (a groan from me at this point)."

As we've mentioned before, the last thing you want is for a stalker to grab your laptop while you're in the restroom in a public place. This happened to me on a cold, foggy morning at Wendy's close to the New Orleans French Quarter. Patrons were few and pigeons were still perched on the wires, as early as it was. Seemed safe enough. No harm in just leaving my laptop running since all I'd intended was to get in and out of the john, right? My bookbag as well was right next to it. You know what happened next.

Next thing I saw when I walked out of the restroom was a ten year old kid in grey sweatpants gunning it for the streetcar that went round to the projects; the *worst* place to chase a thief with a car.

But I was determined to get back, 1.) my laptop and 2.) my bookbag that contained the new shrinkwrapped Elder Scrolls game I'd bought from Babbages. Later I recalled being more concerned with the game, such were my hobbled priorities.

So I used my feet and dashed like the wind, chasing him down Canal Street all the way to St. Charles Ave. When I finally caught up with him, the kid swung and slipped from my grasp like one of those kids in the Philippines who can shimmy up a palm tree in 3 seconds flat to avoid a big cat's teeth. Thankfully, I was the faster one, at least horizontally. He ended up dropping it. My laptop shattered as it hit the concrete. My grip tightened like a vice around his arm. He snarled at me like I was in the wrong.

"Get the hell offa me 'fore I bust yer face!"

He got off lucky, as did I. As he ran down the street flipping me off, I realized that if he'd been a stalker, an ex-flame, and if my laptop had been unencrypted I'd have been toast. He'd have access to:

- My credit cards
- Login passwords for every tech forum under the sun
- Emails
- Amazon, eBay, Google+, Facebook, etc.

The same can happen to you. Worse case scenario: he steals your laptop then leaves it on your doorstep the next morning with an anonymous sticky note. Something about "feeling guilty" - which is a load of bull since your Alienware laptop is now accursed with a keylogger. The kid wants bank account access. Greedy access.

And that's just identity theft. There are other risks, like getting caught trying to preserve invisibility. Some people just like to stay out of the spotlight for whatever reason. By encrypting your laptop, you not only defeat identity thieves, you defeat anyone and everyone that has an interest in seeing you burn.

Tor

I really hate having to insert a bit of overlap here, as some of my other books delve quite deeply into Tor territory. But you just can't write a book on becoming invisible without at least mentioning it. So, here goes.

Tor hides the IP address that websites identify you with. No matter where you go on the internet, if you're not using Tor, you're being tracked somehow by someone, somewhere.

Usually the big name companies like Coke and Dell and Google. The good news is that it's free. As in, really free. No upselling at all as it's not a commercial product. It is *the* app for anonymity enthusiasts and beginners alike. So much so that the NSA targeted it specifically, along with Truecrypt because they were so powerful. So powerful, in fact, that when used together they grant you *complete invisibility* online.

The NSA failed to defeat it. But that didn't stop the FBI from taking a stab at it. They hacked a few websites on the Deep Web by way of browser exploits (or NIT - Network Investigative Technique) that manipulated Javascript to reveal IP addresses. Addresses that lead to your front door. These exploits have been fixed and it's important to note that you don't need Javascript for the internet to work. Some websites, however, won't work. Porn, for example.

Still, after downloading it from the Tor homepage, you need to ensure via the NoScript addon that Javascript is turned off. This will break some websites that use it heavily, like CNN and sites with tons of flash videos. But then if a site is running a dozen scripts it is likely those scripts are tracking you in some way so as to better target you with ads.

Benefits of Tor

1. Immunity to Ad Tracking. What you'll see is ads targeted to some guy in Germany or Japan, since the IP will be that of a Tor user's exit relay (Tor users can volunteer as exit nodes if they wish, but it's not mandatory to use Tor).

2. You can surf the Deep Web, aka .onion sites that are not reachable via the regular internet. The downside is little to no moderation. If you remember how 'Wild West' Usenet was back in the 1990s, you'll have a good idea of what it's like. Freenet is also like that, though it does not connect to the Deep Web in the same way Tor does. In fact, it's a whole different Wild West show, which we will go over shortly.

3. Communicate Anonymously. Using Tor, you can say whatever you want in a forum and not have it traced back to the real You. But don't expect all moderators to not take action to ban your account if you step over the line. Yes, I realize I just contradicted myself here. Perhaps it's better to state that there is little moderation rather than no

moderation on the Deep Web. But what there is, is moderated by lords of the sith in one flavor or another.

4. Upload to file-sharing sites Anonymously. Sites like those owned by the former Megaupload founder. If you need to get something to someone without leaving a trace (even if the zip file is encrypted), such is possible with Tor as long as the website does not block it.

Tails

Tails allows you to use Tor and avoid tracking and censorship and in just about any location you could want. It houses its own operating system and is designed for those who don't wish to use their main rig to connect to Tor (though you still can if you wish).

You've got several choices at your disposal: You can run it via USB stick, SD or even a DVD. This is pretty handy as strengthens your resistance to viruses. It's also beneficial if you don't want your hard drive to leave remnants of your browsing session. The best part is that it's free and based on Linux *and* comes with chat client, email, office, and browser. Everything the anonymity enthusiast needs to wear Frodo's cloak online.

The downside to using a DVD though, is that you must burn it again each time you update Tails. Not very convenient. So let's install it to USB stick instead.

    1.) Download tails installer at tails.boum.org. You must first install it somewhere, like a DVD, and THEN clone it the USB stick or SD card.

    2.) Click Applications --> Tails --> Tails install to begin the installation.

    3.) Choose Clone & Install to install to SD card or USB Memory Stick

    4.) Plug in your device, then scan for the device in the Target-Device drop down menu. You'll get a warning about it overwriting anything on the device, blah-blah. Choose yes to confirm the installation.

Tails by itself is quite a powerful tool to use to cloak yourself online. But when combined with an air-tight and secure operating system like Linux, it is virtually *unstoppable*. If you have the luxury of choosing between vanilla Tor browser in Windows or using Tails, always go with Tails. Windows has always been the favorite whipping boy of the FBI as well as hackers in general, since the number of security holes far outnumber those in Linux.

But Linux doesn't have nearly the amount of supported games. Few supported games = fewer families using it = fewer hackers interested in exploiting it for personal or financial reasons.

VPNs

VPN stands for Virtual Private Network. Great for privacy, lousy for anonymity unless you use it in **conjunction with Tor**. If you want rock-solid privacy and anonymity, then double-wrap.

When I signed up for my first VPN, I was surprised at how easy it was. Almost as easy as signing up with my Usenet provider, Astraweb. Only instead of paying $10/month for newsgroups, you pay $10 for a private connection that masks your IP address. You install the app from the service like CloudVPN and connect through that. The VPN can be from any country, but if you want subpoena-resistant VPN service that approaches anonymity, you better pick a VPN that resides in a country that isn't known for cooperating with U.S. authorities. No, not Iran. Think France, China or Venezuela. It's not 100% subpoena-proof, but luck favors the prepared.

Freenet

The Big Brother of Tor, Freenet, doesn't really hide your IP address. It hides *what you're downloading with your IP address*. Say you want to download a blu-ray movie. There's not many of those on Freenet, but let's say for argument that you had one you wanted to share. You'd install at freetnetproject.org. Then install the Frost frontend addon (discussed below). Then you'd click the upload button which would give you the Chk address you need to share it with others. Then you'd paste the Chk address to one of the hundreds of Freenet groups available.

Benefits of Using Freenet

Chat anonymously. Freenet is known for it's "Darknet" functions that allow complete anonymous communication between two people or even a group. Upon installation, you choose the security level. Low security, in which it is easy for others (with sufficient resources) to find your identity, or high security, in which you only connect to darknet peers - friends you absolutely trust. Your files are still encrypted end to end so that no one knows who uploaded or downloaded what.

Download Anonymously. As stated, anything you downloaded, provided you chose normal security levels at installation, will not be viewable by anyone else because of the end-to-end encryption.

Downsides to Using Freenet

1.) Freenet is SLOW. It is not nearly as fast as Bittorrent or eMule. It takes hours to days to download files a gigabyte in size or higher. Plus, if you've an older PC, it is a bit on the resource-intensive side of things, although anything with an i3 cpu and up will be much faster. That's faster resource-wise, not download speed.

2.) Freenet is complicated. It's not that hard to install and use. It's just hard to find darknet peers you can trust if you want Full Anonymity. The "average" security level is fine for most people, but if you're the leader of a resistance movement in Iran, by all means go perfect dark. Just be certain your darknet peers are 100% trustworthy - a hard feat in this day and age when you've never actually met any of those peers!

3.) Freenet is buggy. It's insanely good at giving you anonymity. Even better than Tor, many say, but you need Java installed for it to work. Because of the sheer complexity of it all, it's not perfect. Yes, Freenet checks whether you have Java on install but even then it occasionally spits out an error if you try to connect. It's usually wrapper-related if on Windows. If this happens, keep trying! Even now, in 2015, I get errors on occasion. I just ignore them and keep hitting 'Connect' until it 'locks on'. Three times is usually enough.

Oh and by the way, never give your Freenet ID to anyone on Freenet. It breaks your anonymity.

Frost

Freenet on its own can be unbearably complex, so I was elated when Frost came around. It's a good front end to make reading groups and downloading CHK files easier.

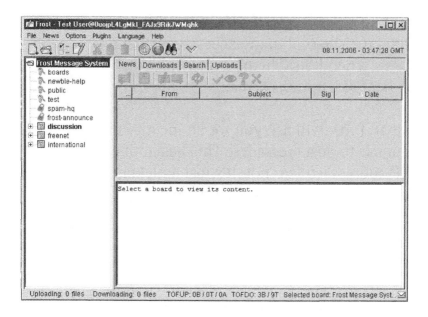

Rest assured, there are many, many groups. You'll have to click the "globe" icon at the top to get a full list, and it will take some time, anywhere from an hour to a day to reveal every single group available.

But first, let's download and install it. It's available at:

http://jtcfrost.sourceforge.net/

Extract the contents into wherever you want to run the application from. If an encrypted container, then you need to have that encrypted container mounted first, then unzip it there.

e.g. Z:\Freenet\Frost

Next create a shortcut to the 'frost.bat' file within. I like to then drag the shortcut to my accessories menu in Windows. Then I disable the annoying splash screen within the Frost options screen.

After that, Frost will ask you for an identity nic, something you can use to post messages. This has nothing to do with your IP address, so fear not. It's just a nickname like you'd use for a Usenet posting in a discussion group.

Options

What I do is go into the News2 section in the options page and check to see if "Hide Messages with Trust States" has "Bad" checked. Then I look at the other option: "Don't add boards to known boards list from users with trust states"... I check off Check, Bad, Observe and None (unsigned) so that I don't end up with boards I don't want in the known boards list. Easy, peasy.

Now then. Look in the News1 section and set the "number of days to display." If you want to see what you missed for the last few months, adjust this number accordingly, to say 300 or however far back you want to download. This is wholly different than Usenet, where a group will go as far back as five years automatically.

Trust

You can control what Frost displays and what it does not. Believe me, this is a godsend when you want to ignore or vet certain users. This is done by way of the trust settings coded into Frost itself.

The options are: Trust, Observe, Check, or Bad. If you mark a user to "Trust," then that person can send you encrypted messages and vice-versa in addition to providing missing blocks of data you might happen to need that this person has. The Observe and Check options are simple: Observe means that I will observe that person's behavior until I can make up my mind on whether to trust him or not. Check is the normal state of trust, meaning no decision's been made on their trust state.

Setting a user's trust to BAD will nuke any posts that person makes on any Frost board. That doesn't mean it's nuked from Freenet, as there is no censorship. It's still there, just invisible to my own eyes. I simply won't see his racist rants (of which there are many on Freenet).

Now then. It could be that we've had conversations on Freenet that we don't want the wife to know about, or the police. I spoke with an attorney on here once and I remember thinking that if ever the police were privy to what went on in that conversation, the jig was up. Over a lousy ticket! They'd know my defense before I could even mount it.

Well. Speaking of mounting, that's something we need to implement: We need to encrypt our operating system, or at least at a minimum, our conversation and preferably our Freenet and Frost installation. We do this by way of encrypted containers. If we're trying to disappear and we need to cross the border for example, what we don't want happening is Mr. Groucho the Canadian Border Guard getting angry about wanting to see what we were talking about in that darknet room. Loose lips and all.

I've been back and forth across the Canadian border more times than I can count, and if there is one thing I've learned, it's that the personality of border guards are notoriously inconsistent across the board. On Monday, you'll get someone with the personality of SuperGrover. That smiley guy could be asked to wear a red cape and he'd salute his superiors and thank them for the great idea. Then on Tuesday you'll get the border guard no one likes to get: a cross between Animal and those two grumpy old farts in the nosebleed section of the Muppet Show. He's the kid who was scarred for life when his mint ice cream cone fell over at Disneyland. And now he takes that trauma out on you!

So with that horrid image out of the way, let's discuss encrypted *containers*.

Counter-Forensics

Encrypted containers are easy to store files in. What isn't so easy is learning the application that enables it. But fear not. Truecrypt took me but a mere weekend to figure out and when I did, I kicked myself for not installing it sooner. I first thought I had to be an advanced coder of some sort to use it. Maybe one of those so-called NSA superhackers we hear so much about. Nope. I was *so* wrong.

If you can install Windows, you can install Truecrypt. Or Veracrypt or Drivecrypt or Diskcryptor or any variation thereof. They all encrypt your files but have different ways of doing it, and many, many apps are available as you'll see. But let's go with the free ones first: Truecrypt and Veracrypt; two excellent choices for us that give a lot of bang for less than a buck.

Truecrypt is first up since the GUI of Veracrypt is practically the same as it's digital brother.

Hold on a second, you say. Isn't the NSA involved in undermining Truecrypt?

Yes and no. It's true that we can see from NSA slides that were leaked that Truecrypt and Tor were in their crosshairs for a long time, but then so is everything else that's tough to crack.

Here's what Veracrypt developers had to say about it. You can interpret it however you wish.

"I am sure the people involved in TrueCrypt couldn't have stayed anonymous and the security agencies knew who they were," he said. "But when you look at the code, you get the idea that these people must have been in their 40s back in 1995. So now they are in their 60s, and they are probably tired or retired."

Truecrypt

There's something else about Truecrypt you might not have heard. It's been discontinued as of 2015, but all the major encryption apps work similarly and it's still secure according to many reliable sources. Once you learn how to use Truecrypt, Veracrypt is a peace of cake. Or you can go ahead and start with Veracrypt in the next section. Your choice.

If you choose Truecrypt, you need to know the basics of creating container files. Once you do that, encrypting the OS is simpler. So, let's create a container file.

Download the app from truecrypt.sourceforge.com and install. Create a container file. Think of it as a treasure chest for which you will create a magic password to open it. Being magic, you wouldn't share that password, right? Right. So never share that password.

Here's a quick rundown:

1. After installation, ensure you have enough free space for your container. How big is the data you're putting inside? Blu-Ray size? Set it accordingly.

2. Select "Create new Volume" from the drop-down menu.

3. Now you have two choices: go the standard route or the double-encrypted treasure chest route (i.e. hidden volume), also called **plausible deniability**. For a beginner, let's go with a simple file container, since hidden volumes require

two passwords and can get a little tricky if you want to store files larger than 4 gigs inside them.

4. You'll soon get to a screen where you have to 'Select File'. Click it. Browse to where you want to store this encrypted container soon to be full of treasure. Don't click on any files yet. Just type in a name in the filename box and choose Save-- We'll add our treasure later.

5. Choose AES for an encryption algorithm. Either is fine but AES has never failed to foil an attacker, because it's super strong. The others get hit with performance penalties on slower systems.

6. Choose the size. Don't select a size too small if you're storing your honeymoon HD videos inside them.

7. Now comes the password. The longer it is and the more random with letters and numbers and symbols, the stronger the entropy, and thus the stronger the pass. Write it down if you must but never forget it. There's no retrieving it if you do.

8. Use your mouse to create a random key, which changes the more you move it. You don't have to do it more than a few seconds. The NSA could spend years and years trying to figure out which direction you moved it first.

9. Now pick a file system, but realize if you're storing big files (4gig and up), you'll need NTFS.

10. You're done! Now just click on the file you initially created. Input the pass, and pick the letter drive you want it

to mount to. Then paste in your videos/documents/treasure. You won't be able to delete this container unless you *unmount* it, which can be done on the Truecrypt screen.

Passwords
At this juncture I should probably answer a question I get quite frequently, which is:

"Help me! I forgot my password but... I know 15 out of the 20 or so character string and in order so... what are my chances of hacking it?"

The answer is: Slim to none, unless you have access to NSA resources, and even that is a long shot for a long password. Encrypted passwords are stored as "hash" files. When you hash a file, even if you change just ONE character in that string, the hash changes. The same is true of jpegs. Throw a picture into Gimp and apply a cool effect or tweak something small and... voila. It's changed. Completely different hash set. Same with encryption.

Evil Maid Attack

Truecrypt, like many other encryption apps, stores your encryption keys in memory ram. A cold boot attack can possibly siphon this if the ram is dumped in the event of a raid or our Jamaican laptop thief gets access to your running operating system. If the former, they can cart off your PC *still running* and freeze the ram sticks *and* dump your keys - which contain your password! The thief, probably not. But an FBI team with a black van parked out front? You can bet the ranch on it.

To that, they are used to all kinds of lowlifes using encryption. Tax evaders. Counterfeit operations. Drug runners. Hells Angels gang members using PGP to communicate where the meth lab is.

The takeaway lesson is this: Don't leave your computer running with any encrypted containers mounted, because it will be dead simple to sniff your passwords from your ram. Unless of course, you break them in half - which in and of itself might be an obstruction of justice charge. Ten years ago this might not have been the case, but the world we now live in is radically different. It demands vigilance on the part of would-be patriots. Always have a plan B.

Drivecrypt - Drivecrypt brings back fond memories. It was my first foray into proprietary encryption apps, and seemed to offer nothing but good things in those early days.

These days though there are a few downsides as technology has progressed about the same rate as exploits in the wild. One is, it's closed source, and at over $100 it's not cheap.

But it's got a great front end and extra goodies if you don't mind paying through the nose. It wasn't for me at the time. For me the bigger issue was: What if the NSA greased Securstar's palms enough (or threatened) to code in a backdoor for the government. If you visit their homepage, you'll see them swear up and down that's not the case. In the end you'll have to decide for yourself whether or not they can be trusted. For what it's worth, they are based in

Germany, not the USA. But if there were a conspiracy then it wouldn't matter which country they operated in.

If you choose yes, know that the demo they offer does not offer strong encryption - only a weak AES key that gets upgraded to full strength if you buy it. I can't recommend Drivecrypt for these reasons:

1. It's closed source.
2. It's pricey.
3. <u>Bruce Schneier</u>, a respected authority on all things security, mentioned in passing after the Snowden leaks that most commercial applications in the USA "...probably have back doors coded into them." Probably, he said, which sounds suspiciously like *certainly* to me. He probably has no more proof of that than I do, but then you don't need to see the code to know using closed-source is a risky endeavor after the NSA (and GCHQ) got caught with their pants down.

<u>Veracrypt</u> - Veracrypt is probably your best bet if Truecrypt has you worried about backdoors. To that, even I had to admit that the account of the strange falling out by the development team had me worried for a time. Rest assured Truecrypt **is** still secure, it's just not **as** secure as other apps, depending entirely on what your security needs are. Plus, later volumes <u>allow you to mount Truecrypt volumes</u>.

So what's so great about it? Well, the developers of Veracrypt emulated the TrueCrypt 7.x code and made it stronger for one thing. Brute forcing is now much more difficult because of the iterations and enhancements added to it. Whenever you encrypt a hard drive partition using Truecrypt, it uses 1000 iterations and 2000 for your containers. But Veracrypt uses a whopping 327,661 of the RIPEMD160 algorithm, which keeps your password and safe contents, well, safe. For encrypted containers? Almost double, at 655,331 iterations of SHA-2 encryption. The only performance penalty comes in at a somewhat slower time to unlock encrypted partitions, a fair tradeoff since it now makes it over three hundred times harder for a hacker to crack by brute force alone.

All of that, plus the user interface looks very similar to Truecrypt, so if you're familiar with that GUI, there's not much of a learning curve at all.

Diskcryptor - With DiskCryptor, you can encrypt any disk partitions or even your main system partition. Being open-source, it was intended as a replacement for Drivecrypt Plus Pack (a commercial closed-source app) and PGP full disk encryption. It supports AES-256, Serpent & Twofish algorithms with the encryption key being stored in the first sector of a volume.

Here's what I found when I compared two different systems:

- SHA-512 hash algorithm in Windows partitions
- Quicker boot than Truecrypt or Drivecrypt Plus Pack
- No mandatory "Create Rescue Disk" like Truecrypt (see workaround)
- Compiles easier than TC.

Cons to Using Truecrypt

1.) It's discontinued. Probably the best reason to use Veracrypt, though it did pass a security audit. DiskCryptor as well does not use the same GUI like Truecrypt does, so you'll have to get used to learning a new one. Not a problem for most but I tend to be stubborn about learning any new GUI.

2.) Limited to RIPEMD-160 hash algorithm for Windows

3.) No support, no future security holes fixed

4.) A few motherboards (Gigabyte's Black Edition line) dislike it.

LibreCrypt - LibreCrypt is open-source disk encryption for Windows, and unlike Truecrypt is LUKS compatible (formerly DoxBox). That's a big plus if you like to dual-boot. Even better is that it supports the same plausible deniability that Truecrypt does. It's listed on the features page as "Deniable encryption that protects you from 'rubber hose cryptography' (snicker!). If you don't know what that is, it's something like this...

Other features are the following:
- Easy to use, with a 'wizard' for creating new 'containers'.
- Full transparent encryption, containers appear as removable disks in Windows Explorer.
- Explorer mode lets you access containers when you don't have administrator permissions.
- Compatible with Linux encryption, Cryptoloop "losetup", dm-crypt, and LUKS.

Linux shell scripts support deniable encryption on Linux.
- Supports smartcards and security tokens.
- Encrypted containers can be a file, a partition, or a whole disk.
- Opens legacy volumes created with FreeOTFE

The rest can be seen at their homepage, at Github.com (search for librecrypt).

CIA Manipulation and Disappearing

There's never been a rack, torture or titillating, that James Bond couldn't get out of and in the most laughable way imaginable. I suppose he's not meant to mirror the real deal, but he's so laser-focused on gadgets that sometimes I wonder if the next villainess that pops out of the cake will come equipped with laser-firing nipples that Bond can dodge in slow motion.

Now, I know as well as you that spies are far from perfect. But it just seems that every Bond film slips a few whoppers where when we least expect it. Suspending disbelief is getting harder to do these days, and here's a few reasons why:

- Guiltless assassination, where a woman can fire seven shots into the ribs of a double-agent and not blink (Mission Impossible: Ghost Protocol).

- Lasers wristwatches that can slice a concrete block in half (Goldeneye).

- A nuke-obsessed madman who carries around the Fancy Feast cat and lives in an underground missile silo. With how often cats get loose from carriers and roam wild in airports, I'd wager it's a good bet that it'd get lost and eventually claw its way to the tip of a nuclear weapon. Mushroom kitty.

To be blunt, the bad guys are far more likely to resemble real-life spies than the good guys. It hurts to think that, let alone say it. It never seems to stop me from liking them any less though, and these days I find myself rooting for them more often than not.

Yep. I root for the bad guys.

That's because they're not only more realistic, but they do far more with far less. Most of them don't make too much noise until the big bang at the end, and they know that mixing sex into the equation is a surefire way to have something blow up in your face. Couple that with the fact that most villains don't think they are villains, and I'll be hooked for two hours.

That said, a lot of methods that involve disappearing into thin air don't quite translate well from the silver screen. In fact the real deal is often not just a *little* different, it's a *lot* different. Bond gets it wrong in almost every film he's in, no matter who plays him or 'Q' or 'M' or even the villain. And Bourne (facepalm), well I do like that the man is being faster on foot and on the draw, but he isn't much better. Like Bond, he attracts too much attention. Far too much.

We see Bond steal a Russian tank and almost single-handedly stop a bullet train and a bomb from going off, with the only snag being his rumpled tie. He almost never takes a bullet, and only smirks as he straightens it his tie and resumes tanking down a busy street. In another film he steals a jet fighter as easily as a cat swipes a smug look off a mouse's face. Just walks right up and bam - off. And none of the dozen or so AK47's firing at the plane prevent a hasty take-off.

I realize I'm picking on Bond perhaps unnecessarily here, but I realize he isn't the only one guilty of exaggeration. Other spy films miss the target. One is True Lies, my all-time favorite.

What you see in True Lies, for example, usually results in a CIA agent shaking his head and leaving his theater seat. I experienced this first hand once, way back in 1994.

Curiously, I left my seat for a Coke refill and followed the man that'd gotten up in a huff and, feigning boredom, I stood as close as I could to better hear what he was mumbling about. Only I couldn't quite decipher it. It was like hearing an asylum patient mumble half-formed questions and who gave himself half-cocked answers. Strange. Then he lit up a cigarette near the concession. I swear, he looked just like Cigarette Man from the X-Files who's always taunting Mulder.

I coughed and asked him why he left during such an incredible scene (where Arnold chases a terrorist up to the Marriot Hotel roof). He asked me the same. I said I'd already seen it a dozen times. As it turned out, he seemed to know more about lies and spies than the producers did. Certainly more than James Cameron. As we got to talking, I was quite blown away by the intel he was generous enough (and perhaps foolish enough, since he smelled like Southern Comfort) to drop about his old line of work: Spycraft.

He said that intelligence work is just not done the way we'd just seen on the silver screen, if ever. If it is, then someone's screwed up somewhere along the way. And often in an unrecoverable way. Neither Bond nor Arnold would've ever lasted half as long as they did if it were real life. I knew that much. He then said the guy'd be axed long before he wound up dead, and they'd give him a gift of hair gel mixed with gasoline as a farewell present for the embarrassment he caused them. I almost laughed but stopped myself. I'd no idea if he was serious or not.

He went on. CIA techniques, he said, use a lot of deception; deceiving the target's mind with a lot of psychology and lies and well-timed poker faces. When the time is right, they attack. They steal what they need to... and that's it. No stolen nukes or radioactive goo or bombs set to go off 5 minutes after you get it. No Swiss estate going boom with guard dogs leaping at the last minute only to have Arnold bash their heads together midair.

"Well, it's only a movie after all," I recall saying. "We're supposed to suspend belief y'know." I knew all about suspension of disbelief and prepared to lecture him on this lost art.

He cut me off and laughed just as he waved away little puffs of cigarette smoke.

"But they always, without fail, half-ass the research. They half-ass everything, I'm telling you." He took a long drag and stared in the direction of what I guessed was Russia. "Cameron no doubt wrote that crap on a napkin in his hospital robe with a case of the runs. I read that somewhere."

I tried not to laugh. Even now, he sounds angrier on paper than he really was. But I knew I'd feel the same if I'd seen my line of work cheapened like a Michael Bay flick. I still loved the movie, though, flaws and all. But I always hated Michael Bay's movies.

The gist of that conversation, however, was that no matter which decade you're in, good spying and by extension, *disappearing*, relies on <u>intense networking</u>. And not only that, but intense analyzing and tracing and focusing - all until you get as much data as you can on your enemy, and all while being as quiet as a church mouse. Kinda like most of Bond's villains, come to think of it.

You have to admit, that's pretty boring material to work with if you're James Cameron. If you recall the scene in True Lies where the camera pans over a snowy Swiss estate patrolled by six fur-coated razor blades, you remember how cool it looked for a guy as big as Arnold to get in there so effortlessly and leave with nary a scratch. Then not long after we see him waltz right out the front gate and... BOOM. The place blows up like Chernobyl. And all after doing the Tango with Tia Carrere. Running time: less than 5 minutes.

And all for a lousy computer file that could've easily been accessed offsite if the van hacker was half as good as he sounded.

At any rate, I learned that you do learn a lot of survival techniques that, for a few moments, might resemble something Arnold did on a bad hair day in Switzerland. But it's very, very rare.

If it comes down to you chasing a terrorist through New York traffic and riding a horse to the top of the Marriott with him taking a flying leap for the pool one hotel over, you can forget about getting any recognition for that on the inside. You're being sloppy, and your supervisor just may send you to Alaska for a year to cool your jets. The visibility factor alone would make world headlines. If you learn anything from social media sites, you know that attention whoring usually means failure. It's doubly true offline.

Manipulation Tactics

The manipulation methods used by the CIA are nothing new. Back when I ran online ad campaigns (my first business failure), I manipulated people left and right without even realizing it. Every day.

I'd fire up CPV Lab on my server and spend (and lose) thousands running ads for affiliate companies like Neverblue and Clickbank, while buying traffic from TrafficVance and LeadImpact. It was all hellishly confusing, and never cheap.

But once in a blue-moon, I'd split-test two ads enough to see my sales skyrocket. At that point, I was *hooked*. And quite stunned at what a little tweak here and there via manipulation could accomplish. It felt like cheating to be honest. And dirty. Like that used car salesman from True Lies and his phony spy cover to bang chicks in his souped-up Ferrari.

Though I never made enough for a Ferrari, I knew it was effective manipulation and strangely enough, legal. That's the part that took me a long time to get; that giving people what they think they need in exchange for something I *wanted*, was at least morally speaking, a grey area. Sort of. I guess it depends on which side of the political aisle you're on, but it did pay for tuition and felt great to think of myself as a budding businessman. Later I began to realize a few truths.

Corporations do this all the time; Sears. Target. Wal-Mart. Best Buy. They're artists at it. But what works in the USA may not work in Canada; like Target thinking that customers in the USA were clones of Canadians. They found out the hard way that manipulation works differently in different cultures as much as Bond's weapons work differently when he's in 'Q's lab and shooting it out on a zero-G space station in Moonraker.

The point is this: You needn't hesitate to manipulate someone if it's required to maintain your cover, regardless if you're in Bangkok or Montreal or New Orleans. If more good'll come from you being invisible than being exposed, all the better. A good CIA agent will have zero problems with manipulation if it means it'll push the mission objective *forward*. Best Buy does this, and they have pretty atrocious pricing on many items not the least of which is the worthless extended warranty they pressure you into buying. I've been suckered for years to buy those things.

So why then, do more people shop there instead of a smaller PC repair shop? The answer is manipulation. P.T. Barnum called it 'being suckered!'

This doesn't mean you have to be a lying, two-faced brown-noser. It just means that you need to know how to manipulate without giving valuable intel about your past away. For therein is the art of the disappearing act.

Forging Alliances

The CIA doesn't like sowing bad seeds.

Bad seeds usually mean enemies at some point in the future. They prefer to make *allies*, even if those allies aren't exactly shining examples of virtue. An alliance is good enough, they figure, if the benefits outweigh the costs.

What does that mean for you? Well it means good alliances can be beneficial no matter where you forge them. The CIA certainly knows this. To this end, they spend tons of money and manpower that are devoted to finding at least *some* common ground with enemies, then accelerate common goals before parting ways and becoming hardcore enemies again. It's all a feedback loop of deceit, but many times it works and works very well. They learn a lot about these pseudo-enemies. It all sounds rather counter-productive, and it can be until you realize how much misinformation the good guys give to the bad guys.

Thereafter, and only thereafter, will they send in the spies - once they truly have undermined the enemy in as deceitful way as possible.

The Soviets preferred this method, only their methods were far darker in the implementation. They had no qualms about offing civilians or kids or beloved pets or even priests. It really mattered little what it was that got under people's skin, for as long as it drove them to fight each other, that was good enough.

KGB defector Yuri Bezmenov relayed this brilliantly, and perhaps as ominously as Jonah did to the inhabitants of Ninevah. He laid it out like a strategic battle plan in his "Love Letter to America," how everything the KGB did to undermine western democracy and freedom as you know it was put above all else, even their own citizens.

An interview he gave in 1983 was quite telling, and even shocking in some parts of the telling; How the Russians would invite a U.S. diplomat to mother Russia, get them drunk, plastered, pickled and primed for a lie, then paint a rosy picture of how pretty and flowery Russia was - both the people and her politicians. Only it wasn't. Even Ted Kennedy bought it.

Prisons were turned into nurseries overnight. Spies and liars tricked every reporter that came around shooting for LIFE and Time. Magazine spreads portrayed the entire country as victims of the evil U.S. capitalistic empire, yet Russia bore it all with smiling faces and vigorous "happy" handshakes living under the benevolent Soviet government.

Only we know how *that* story ended. The Soviet Union broke up and went into a death spiral. The lesson here for anyone contemplating disappearing in a free country is this: Have Ethics.

Have a moral base and keep your manipulation tactics sane so that, heaven forbid you are caught red-handed, you won't be strung up from the nearest tree by your compatriots for going too far. Sew your relationships to your advantage, certainly, but don't sacrifice your soul to do so.

How The NSA Finds Anyone

Predictability [pri-dik-tuh-bil-i-tee] Noun - *The consistent repetition of a state, course of action, behavior, or the like, making it possible to know in advance what to expect.*

Predictability is a trait the NSA relies on to track people effectively without meeting any surprises later on. And not only the NSA in the States, but intelligence agencies across the *entire* globe. Without it, any mass surveillance is pretty much like targeting plastic decoy ducks bobbing around in a pond. Given enough time, a duck will sense when it's being targeted unless the hunter changes his strategy.

But one thing he must never do is become predictable. Ducks aren't the smartest birds out there, but they catch on pretty quick when something's up. The trick of the trade is to counter their instincts with knowledge - knowing their habitat and weaknesses before the hunt ensues.

Likewise, the NSA also depends on your weaknesses. They've tools that expose your weaknesses, too, and tools like zero-day exploits in your own phone that help their team of superhackers predict where the prey (you in this case) is going to be, and all with a laser-like precision that's tough as nails to deflect, unless you yourself can predict where they'll look.

You probably guessed cell towers help them out a lot in this regard, and you'd be right. But cell towers only go so far. Sometimes, the NSA calls for help from local and state law enforcement to spy on suspects. Suspects like double-agents, for instance, but those local guys only like to help if there's something in it for them. Something that makes good headlines; nice flashy headlines that plead for public funding or else thousands of innocent children holding fluffy kittens will be killed by a meteor storm.

Eventually, the public gets worked into a frenzy and the next thing you know, you'll catch your local congress-critter voting to divert funds to the NSA, but only under the cover of night. By the time the local populace finds out, it's too late to reverse the tide because the tsunami's here - in all it's watery horror and there's little that'll benefit you unless you turn tail and run for the hills. People who fight against it before it gets anywhere *near* the beach are labeled extremists or alarmists or some other 'ist' that carries a negative panicky vibe.

So how does the NSA get away with it?

From *you*.

Yes, the biggest aid to the NSA in spying on the citizenry... is the citizenry itself! And the citizenry's been too soft in recent years. As a social whole they don't like ruffling the feathers of the mama duck watching all the baby ducks. They're afraid of what's out there. Boogey-foxes who eat ducks, I suppose, or perhaps freezing to death or sinking or drunkenly waddling into a portal that leads to a planet of duck-eating zombies. Who knows. Everybody's different. Only they'll never know for sure because more than a few ducklings *like* the idea of a Big

Mama watching their every move. Except by not looking right under their nose, they failed to see the water moccasin coming in quick for the kill!

Which brings us back to predictability.

Becoming unpredictable on a personal level is uncomfortable. It makes noise to unravel it and rewire your hardwired habits again. It requires work. Hard work. Most people don't like to rub two brain cells together to fight off the tsunami unless they can see it from the beach - from safety.

Think about it. You wake up at the same hour and in the same place every day. You wear the same style of clothes every season. Shop at the same retail outlets. Visit the same places come Memorial Day. Date the same type of people, even if they aren't your dream dates (for me, redheaded librarians with glasses). Married people? Forget it. You're not getting off the NSA radar without taking the fight to them, and that's a fight that requires getting out from under her wing. It also involves significant risk. But there are ways to get around it...

Cell Towers

Cell phone networks are a bit like computers in that they need to know *where you are* in order to "talk" to you. Networked computers, too, need IP addresses. Without them there's *zero* communication since it has nowhere to send the data packets. It's the same with cell networks. Cell geolocation is a requirement to send you your stuff.

Skype, emails, Warcraft pings. Things like that. It doesn't really matter what kind it is, but one thing that's for certain is that *the NSA prefers you favor convenience over security,* since breaching security is harder for them.

If millions of people put convenience above security, that's all the more power for them. They win and you lose. If the reverse is true, then they'd have a real problem on their hands.

Triangulation isn't really anything new. It's just that now they've refined it, looped it, hacked it and manipulated it in such a way that it's now infused with emergency services, with we the little people being like a hiker's dog that gets stuck in a cliff crevice with no way back up. Once the slippery slope takes effect, it's almost impossible to get ourselves back to where we were originally.

There are other crusty old bones to worry about, like passwords and cell phone security within text messaging apps. One reason these apps are so popular is because of their simplicity. Even that crusty old Uncle Spanky can use it. But if Uncle Spanky sends his password through his cell phone in a text message, his security's cooked!

The reason for this is that text messaging works like email. After your phone relays it to a distant server, it must look up where to send it. That is, the *destination* point, which'll be on a different carrier's network. There, it'll get frisbeed into a mailbox until such time as the other person's phone retrieves it.

Now, at any point in time *after* it does this, there's a number of risks that can come into play.

A hacker may snipe it. It could bounce somewhere longer than you intended. It could be manipulated by the cops, the NSA or even Chinese programmers with too much time on their hands. These days even Google is suspect with the absurd amount of subpoenas they get every day.

When you get right down to it, there's an infinite number of destinations where it could wind up, and all on account of Uncle Spanky trusting his phone implicitly. So if you're reading this Uncle Spanky, if you've not developed proper security mindset (the kind we talked about at Pat O'Briens in the French Quarter) to ensure you *never* send clear text unsecured, then your clear text will always become *compromised* text. Every time.

(and if Uncle Spanky remembers that conversation, I'll die a happy man).

At any rate, that's just one way in which cell towers can kill your privacy.

'But hold on," you say. Why should *I* care about a secure level of anonymity if I'm doing nothing illegal? I don't deal drugs. I don't hire contract killers to snipe Betsy in HR who flipped me off in traffic the other day. I'm also not a bank robber like one of those guys from Heat, so what's the big deal? I don't care if the NSA or Goober from Mayberry reads an email I sent last year.

Well the deal is this: How would you feel if your house was transparent, and everyone could take video of you singing in the shower? How about if they streamed it to every tube site on the internet?

Or what if a person wants to lawyer up a last will and testament? Let's say they want to specify that they don't want so much as a grain of sand in their vast estate (an estate that took decades to build) going to their idiot cousin Neb; Neb who not only likes torturing small animals, but whose expert critique of anything political or scientific is comprised of his favorite four words: 'I think it's stupid!'

Do you think he'd want the whole world knowing? Of course not. Any business that you or anyone else decides to build (writing for example), should come with a right to privacy, unless you've signed it away beforehand.

Long before the internet became mainstream, this was all but guaranteed. Back in the 1980s, police needed a search warrant before they could rifle through your private things and wiretaps were hard to get. In those days, you were innocent -until- proven guilty. Today, with technology being propped up on a pedestal as a human right, our human rights, ironically enough, have gone out the window. We've actually *lost* rights because of the near-lightspeed advance of technology, which sad to say, is not compatible with the tortoise-speed evolution of law enforcement and intelligence agencies like the NSA. Outside of the military, the tendency in government jobs is to do the least amount of work possible. In technology, it's the reverse since the tech seems to evolve on its own.

Regardless, if you're using PGP, you should never be considered a criminal simply because you use it and must have something to hide. You could be communicating with your son who is part of a resistance movement in Iran. Or planning a surprise anniversary event for your spouse. Does it matter what it is? What matters is that you have ultimate control of what's inside Pandora's Box, and other, more powerful agencies don't, a fact they don't like. When push comes to shove, it's liberty vs. tyranny.

Take the U.S. Congress for example. Future congresses are not bound to the laws of our present Congress. They can change it at will in the cover of darkness if they wish, much like the Canadian Parliament backstabbed millions of Canadians with the FATCA deal with the U.S. (giving the IRS permission to peek into their savings accounts). They can switch up the rules without any pressing questions from the media. Can you adapt to the new government's rules on a whim? The same government that you never liked but voted for anyway for a little bit of security... after they formed a coalition?

From the EFF's privacy page:

Privacy rights are enshrined in our Constitution for a reason — a thriving democracy requires respect for individuals' autonomy as well as anonymous speech and association. These rights must be balanced against legitimate concerns like law enforcement, but checks must be put in place to prevent abuse of government powers.

Giving powerful agencies the freedom they now demand from us would never be enough. They'd always want more. They can evolve and take over things gradually in the same way a cancer does when it invades a cell. One piece at a time. One organelle at a time. One organelle is never enough and neither is one cell. They'll attack other cells that pass by. Pretty soon the following occurs:

- Every ISP knows every click you make.
- Every website you visit is cataloged.
- Every international internet user you speak with, Skype with, flirt with, is recorded.
- Every business monitored. Every cent paid. You walk by it and glance over, they know about it.
- Every extra 'carbon footprint' you take - recorded and if severe enough, fined.

Therefore, encryption and anonymity are mandatory lessons you must learn unless you want the future to be comprised of:

- Transparent envelopes.
- Cams in your home, your bathroom, your pool, your pet.
- Transparency in clothes (subject to approval by some bureaucrat)

- Transparency in cars - driven by the State or worse, Google.

If the above ever comes to fruition, citizens may begin to not only observe what is legal or quasi-legal, but live their lives in as Pharisee mentality as possible if for no other reason than to not get flagged for helping a brother out of a pit.

Drones (and How to Defeat Them)

Above, a U.S. Customs Patrol Drone at more than 5000 feet up.

If you're trekking across the border and wondering whether or not you'll see a drone 20,000 feet up, relax. Chances are good that you won't. It isn't just the sheer height of the blasted things that are the problem. It's how easily Mother Nature tends to obscure their flight patterns with things we can't control.

Things like clouds, fog, and thunderstorms.

These acts of God make a lot of anti-drone technology an exercise in frustration. As well, they're soundless for the most part. Soundless, silent killers in the night sky, the twinkling of which you could easily mistake for a star. Could you tell the difference? I couldn't when I tried.

But let's not fall on our swords just yet, for there are a few measures we can employ should that day of reckoning ever surface. Measures that require technical aptitude and good ole fashioned common sense can be a godsend if you think ahead of time.

1.) <u>Sensor Disruption</u> - Any technology with sensors needs to see the target it's trying to capture. So any good patriot needs to give it a dose of it's own medicine:

That medicine is LASERS.

Have you ever wondered why a kid with a laser pointer gets a visit from the FBI after he points it at a 747 flying overhead? And so quickly? That's because they know the exact angle and coordinates from which the laser came from. And it's not as if the things are harmless, either.

Lasers disrupt not only the instruments onboard, but the visibility of the pilots. Blind pilots cannot fly straight, nor can they read their navigation systems for as long as that kitty laser is bouncing around the cockpit. And there may just be several of them being pointed by giggling schoolgirls at a slumber party on Friday night.

It's the same with drones, and though pilotless, they've cameras that relay images to a set of human eyeballs. Clever anti-surveillance groups may even set up auto-targeting turrets that flash lasers constantly at an approaching drone. The downside to doing this is that you give up your location unless you set the device a significant distance from your base of operations.

2.) <u>Hacking</u> - This one's far easier said than done. It used to be that drones could be hacked just as flight navigation systems on a 747 could be hacked, but it's harder to do now since many are encrypted. The movie Interstellar goofed on this point. In the film, we see Matthew McConaughey helping his daughter hack into a drone flying overhead. He makes it all look so simple, kinda like the other Matthew did in Wargames. That's because there was no encryption to hack.

Years prior to the film's release, North Korea and Iran both claimed to have downed drones using hacking techniques, whereby they 'spoof' the GPS signal and send it on a suicidal death spiral. There is a longish guide below if you're curious as to what it'd take to bring one down.

http://privat.bahnhof.se/wb907234/killuav.htm

3.) <u>EMP Pulse</u> - The problem with this attack is that even if you could create this by yourself, the pulse cares not a whit about your own electronic equipment or grid. It'd be shooting yourself in the foot. Actually, a little worse. Recall the MAD tactic (mutually assured destruction) Trinity used in The Matrix just as the A.I machines began to drill into Morpheus' ship, The Nebuchadnezzar - with Neo and Morpheus still jacked in. She hit the switch and fried every bot in range but left her ship a sitting duck.

4.) <u>Counter-Drones</u> - This requires downed drones unless you can manufacture your own. Set these drones to survey the skies for unfriendlies and scan and identify via encryption keys the same way that PGP users do over the internet. The primary issue is that the enemy can see these just as you can see their own drones - unless you've got decoys set up to give off fake heat signatures.

5.) <u>Occupy The High Ground</u> - For this to work, you need teams specially trained and camouflaged to stand watch on the lookout for drones all day, all night, armed with microwave-type weaponry. You'd also need powerful scopes to distinguish a drone from a plane, which is not discernable to the naked eye even from high up. Noise sensors would be required that detect the low-hum engine noise from a drone, which assumes you know the make/model of the drone you're targeting.

6.) <u>Camouflage</u> - I don't mean the Ghillie suit used in Call of Duty, but rather the natural camouflage given by large structures. Shadows, bridges covered in vines, that sort of thing. Only traveling at night is risky no matter what you wear since the drone can detect your heat signature better than most other machines. Therefore if at any time you find yourself being targeted, it's best to stick to tunnels, under bridges, railroad tracks and move building to building, cover to cover.

If you can blend in with what the drone considers 'non-adversarial' structures, then it won't distinguish between you and Vladmir. The real threat is the facial recognition technology it may use, where it can match your face with a database and cross-reference it with fingerprints. The old methods work, but so do the old solutions: If you're a wanted man, wear a hood, makeup, beard or whatever you need to look thinner or fatter than you really are.

That also goes for your <u>voice</u>. Voice DNA's come a long way, so if you find yourself in Ukraine and running from a lush forest into a small hick town, you better know the accent. The language in Kiev is not the same as in Moscow, just as Montreal French isn't the same as Paris French. Little mistakes can give up the golden goose. More on this later.

7.) <u>Radar</u> - The expensive option, but at thirty thousand feet you're probably not going to see a drone without expensive equipment, and if you're being bankrolled by a powerful resistance group, well then you might as well go all the way. Right to the end of the line.

Something to note here, that even if you were to step outdoors and see a trail from a jet liner, it'll be as a tiny sliver on a clear, sunny day. Rain and fog can be a problem, so you need radar installations that are secret enough to evade enemy detection, but *close enough* to *see* the enemy. As you can imagine, it's quite the Catch-22. Detecting the drone comes far easier than detecting it anonymously.

8.) <u>Civilian Patriots</u> - Obvious perhaps, as there are over a million gun owners in the U.S. and Canada combined. Asking a survival forum what the chances of a rogue government or police state has of using them successfully on an armed populace is like jumping into a creation/evolution debate. By page 200, no one's mind is ever changed. I'll state that it's unlikely that drones will be turned against the populace anytime soon in a violent manner, because they must be rearmed and refueled, and a patriotic force would seize this opportunity to string the pilots up from the nearest tree. That is, if they ever found the base doing it. I've a hunch they'd find them very quickly.

When all is said and done, a *spying drone* is different than a *firing drone*. And in the end, perhaps that is really all they want; to launch a hundred thousand drones to spy on everyone without ever firing a shot. Because when you know where someone is 24/7, what restaurant they eat at, what ballgames they attend and can see from the skies whether they put their ketchup on top of their fries or on the side, they don't really need to fire from up there, do they?

Bin Laden's Courier and the Art of Staying Invisible

Sheikh Abu Ahmed wasn't an easy man to find. The CIA spent an entire year tracking him down. Thanks to Bin Laden's rule of no cell calls or laptops, it made it all the more difficult. So difficult in fact, that they had to rely on getting intel out of prisoners.

The big break came in 2010 when Ahmed broke Bin Laden's rule by dropping his name on, you guessed it, a cell phone. Intelligence agencies had already monitored the contact and when Bin Laden's name dropped, the call led them straight to the isolated Pakistani town of Abbottabad. You probably know already how the raid went down.

Navy SEALs stormed the compound not long after. The 18 foot walls and barbed wire did nothing to stop them. It was lightning fast, too. In and out in under 40 minutes, and with so little resistance it became apparent that overconfidence was not only the courier's weakness, but Bin Laden's as well. There were no guard towers or tight schedules to monitor. No Rottweilers or German shepherds and no field of trip mines and no Barrett guns to worry about. Generally speaking, a light infantry unit could've done him in just as easily.

There's a good opsec lesson that we can learn from the raid. The first lesson is easy to grasp: Never draw attention to yourself by being **loud**. If you want to truly disappear without problems popping up later, we need to ignore not only bar braggarts, but mentioning details about your past in *any* setting.

As well, avoid loud, boisterous people. Blabbermouths. Gossip rags. Drama queens. Bin Laden, for all his demonic activity, had this part right. He not only avoided loud people but avoided loud *explosions*.

You'd think he'd have planted C4 in the surrounding fields. He didn't.

Why not? Because its terribly loud and draws too much attention. Same with mines which can be counter-productive. Tripwires can kill your own guys and put you on the radar of the local police. Sentry guards can be seen from the sky. They're also as loose-lipped as a group of old church ladies when they get bored of walking the same beat day in, day out. Gossip kills time, which in turn kills operational security like nothing else.

Sometimes Hollywood gets it wrong. Those SEALS (the real ones) knew how to be silent. In fact, it's the very thing they do best as most missions rely on radio silence to limit exposure. The aim is to get in and out and *then* blow the place sky high, after which you can run to the beach blabbing to your teammates as much as you want. But if there's one thing that'll put a silver bullet in your disappearing act, it's blabbing about your old life.

"I sure showed the IRS! Those turkeys won't bother me ever again!" you might say just a little too loudly in a Bangkok bar. Little did you know however that there's a vacationing IRS agent a few chairs down.

There are other rules we need to follow other than simply keeping our mouth shut. One involves restriction. That is, restricting who may peek into our private life.

Restrict Physical Access

Never trust anyone with your laptop overseas. Admittedly this is a pretty broad brush to stroke with, but whenever something bad happened to me like theft or identity fraud, nine times out of ten it involved me loaning my laptop to someone I'd known less than a month. If you absolutely must loan it out, ensure that you are present *as they are using it.*

How come?

Because inside your laptop lies the heart and soul of not only your business, but your entire life. Break it off with a vengeful girlfriend and she can do a lot more than just the battery-acid-to-the-face to the other girl. She can ruin you as well and make getting a credit card or laptop replacement a nightmare.

Encrypt your hard disk at a bare minimum. That means everything: Your files. Your forums. Your passport. Anything that is linked to you can be used against you. Now, you needn't go as far as Bin Laden did and avoid laptops altogether since that'd be pretty overkill for your needs, but you definitely want to limit the damage any single person can do.

This is especially important if you're a freelancer, an author, or just have an online side hustle. Guard those passwords and pen names as though they opened the doors to Heaven itself!

Hell hath no fury gents, and that goes double for strangers. By strangers I mean anyone you've known less than three months. The last thing you need is a string of fake reviews from people who have never read anything by you.

If you need covert-level anonymity, then don't give out your real last name. It's sounds extreme because it is. But extreme security means taking extreme precautions. Plus, it means not letting any kind of ID, international or otherwise, fall into anyone else's hands. It also means:

- Storing passports, driver's licenses, etc., in a combination lockbox or safe out of sight at the hotel or apartment. Somewhere high up. Like an AC vent.

- Never carry your passport on you. A copy is good enough, but alter the last name.

- Never mention forums you visit, nor usernames. Take Ars Technica for instance. If your avatar for your Windows lock screen is the same as your forum avatar, she may stumble upon it and see every post you've ever made. Disastrous!

Preserving Your Reputation

If you've ever seen the Game of Thrones HBO show, then you know how merciless the author is with his characters. I watched in horrific amazement how brutal the deaths were. Even a horse was decapitated.

But I pressed on, week after week, until they finally killed off Ned Stark, the Hand of the King. I began to think Sean Bean was contracted to be killed off in every film he's in.

I sat it out for a month after Season 1 just to figure out why the author was so brutal to his fans. A little while later, I decided to come back (rather foolishly, in hindsight) and resumed watching right up until the Red Wedding. It was a bloodbath. Evil Dead was never so gruesome.

After that monstrosity, I hatched a scheme of hunting the author down with a rather twisted colleague of mine. That colleague is a genius when it comes to pranks, some of which can be quite shocking. The plan was to persuade the author to sign a Game of Thrones book in a fan's own blood.

We chickened out. Or rather, *I* chickened out, as soon as we saw him. What scared us off the idea was not the security the man had, but the frenzy of fans that adored the very air molecules the man breathed. I envisioned the worst kind of butchery would befall us if we insulted him. Like torch and spears and being strung up from the nearest tree butchery.

One lesson I learned was that there's a lot to be loved about Game of Thrones that don't involve violence. One is the characters.

If there's one thing that runs throughout every season of Game of Thrones, it's that reputation is everything. One line in particular housed this idea perfectly. It's a line from Tyrell Lannister, the dwarf son of the new hand of the King; a master at deceit and a whoremonger of the lowest sort. A guy that somehow manages to steal every single scene he's in as well. Oh, and he has the best lines, one of which is:

"A Lannister always pays his debts."

It's mostly used in a negative context, and while not completely original, it's royal wisdom housed in six little words can save your life someday. I'm speaking of course of local debts. Friendship debts. Family business debts. Loan sharks. Not: Student loans, credit cards and mortgages. For these you can always hire a lawyer.

Getting into debt in a Wild West place like Pattaya or Manila can make enemies *faster* than a drunk Lannister stabbing a dagger onto a buffet table and threatening to give the boy king a wooden johnson.

There, they can be even more merciless than any tyrant - right as you dismount your rented motorbike in the light of day. Perhaps even outside your hotel. You'll never see it coming if you get too deep into debt (or jealousy as the case may be in the Philippines).

These same sort of enemies can pour a can of puke-green paint all over your invisibility act and destroy everything you've built up to that point. The problem is that you never quite know what foreign men or women are capable of, and you don't have ten years to 'get to know' *what* they're capable of because you'll know soon enough if you become indebted to them.

Cut Them Loose

This means cutting loose someone who has proven to be unstable and detrimental to *your* stability. It can go up in smoke in a pinch. Financially unstable people tend to borrow without asking and make an awful lot of assumptions about your generosity.

There's a few strategies we can use for disarming these kind of people, and by extension, preserve our privacy and way of life.

<u>One requires saying no</u>. In some cases, it requires *firing* someone in your life who makes a lot of noise flapping their gums or causes other mischief. A maid with sticky fingers, for example, can be catastrophic but still be easier to fire than your live-in girlfriend. Better to suffer a bruised ego for a day than lose a business and a year's worth of new clients.

Before I traveled abroad, a friend warned me about mixing romance and business. You may be asked to bring a gift to the family *before* you can take her out to a nice restaurant. Even then, it'll be with Uncle Wang as date chaperone.

"Can't you afford it?" she'd slyly asked. "Sure can," came the reply. But I'm not your walking white ATM and you're no Princess Diana, so... ciao."

Five years prior I'd have felt bad about hurting her feelings. But by being bold, matching their boldness with my own, I spared myself the expense of buying *all* her relatives electronic gadgets that might've cost $300-400 per item... on all future engagements. Later I found this to be common no matter where one might be in the Philippines. If you're there, you're one rich cowboy since the plane ticket alone is four figures and most Pinoys know it.

As in, Bill Gates rich. So learn to say no, but do so prior to disappearing in any country, hurt feelings or not.

Risky Friendships

When you are a stranger in a strange land, it can be tempting to accept any and all friendships that fall into your lap. And believe you me, they'll come and come quick with you being the new face in town. People like allies. Allies make strong families stronger. But a few of them just want to see what your financial worth is.

You'll also catch stares in places you've never dreamed of: The Mall. The Parks. The Marina. Renting a motorcycle? Yep, plenty of stares there. They're all wondering why you're not buying the blasted thing since, you know, you're as rich as Bill Gates.

Then there's your shiny new identity. You'll feel more alive than ever before. No debts. No criminal past. No angry ex looking to string you up from the nearest tree if you don't fork over two grand by the end of the month for her maintenance lifestyle. Onlookers will swear you've got a glow and Peter Pan's worry-free shadow following you around.

Then comes the kicker: you meet someone at a convention and offer a beer after you forge a connection. He smiles with a row of perfect teeth, nods and hmms and offers expert marketing advice. You think, "Gee, this guy seems like a pretty smart guy. He's got a real knack for business. Cool. Bet'd he'd make a great business partner, too, for my new coffee entrepreneurship."

After all, what digital nomad doesn't want new clients and new allies?

Only later, you find out he runs a tranny dating website for Thais and wants you to "meet someone to discuss better ways to attract clientele." I'm sure you know the risks of such a scenario.

Snowden's Mistakes

Edward Snowden. He's an interesting character study in how far a guy will go on personal ethics alone.

He gave up a six-figure salary. U.S. citizenship. Passport. Then as if that weren't enough, he stoked the fury of the very powerful U.S. elite in leaking classified NSA documents that proved without a doubt that Americans were being spied on relentlessly. Whether you agree or disagree with the traitor label, I believe we can agree that it took a measure of courage (or insanity) to do what Snowden did.

He'd insisted from the very beginning that the NSA's surveillance programs were in violation of the U.S. Constitution, and that the descendants of the Constitution's founders deserved to know about them. Nothing good, he said, ever came from keeping tax-funded programs in the dark from the taxpayers themselves. They needed to know one way or another, what their money was funding and who was responsible.

No one knows if he'll be forgiven someday by his critics. Neither does anyone know for certain what any future Congress is capable of. But if there's one thing that *is* certain, it's that they can change laws retroactively. Yep, retroactively. It's an immense power that demands balance. What balance? The balance that prevents a tyrannical government from assuming power. Simple concept, right? Only nothing is simple when our congress critters are in session, and I've no doubt that the Weimar Republic had some primitive data collecting scheme in place long before Hitler came rose to power. We only saw bits and pieces of it along the way.

"I did this to give the American people a chance to decide for themselves what type of government they want to have. That is a conversation that I think the American people deserve to decide."

Those were Edward's words to the American people. Words that fell on many deaf ears. It's a sad fact of life that no prophet was ever accepted in his own hometown. Those were Christ's words. And I believe that just as we can learn from Christ, we can learn from the Snowden, or at the very minimum, his mistakes.

Mistake #1: Moscow

It was WikiLeaks founder Julian Assange that provided for Snowden's stay in Hong Kong, even recommending that he not go to South America on account of the physical danger to himself. It wasn't as if the place was paradise, since the general instability of the area makes for a miserable experience in a lot of cities, cartels included.

But as luck would have it, he ended up in Russia when his passport was yanked.
And it isn't even what Snowden *said* that is most appealing to the Russians. Rather, it's what he didn't say; that unwritten, unspoken matrix of secrets swimming around in his head that are a veritable *gold mine* for Russian Intelligence. It's a good bet that if Washington ever offers him a plea deal and allows him back on American soil, we'll see the same stalling behavior we saw with Vladimir Putin's decision. They won't give him up so easily.

The worst mistake you could ever make would be to hop a plane to a destination you know little about. Finance is the first obstacle. Then culture. Then language. Know where you want to run and why you want to run there and badger yourself with questions until you're blue in the face.

Is it safer than neighboring countries? Any extradition treaties? Can you open a bank account there from your home country... without leaving a trace? You need to know all of this well before you make a move.

With the kind of security clearance Edward had, getting a second passport in a country friendly to the United States should have been easy peasy. Sure, said country may have handed him over without hesitating, but not without at least a delay that might have granted him more time. When you're on the run from a superpower, time is worth more than pink diamonds. And any 1st world government will know it if you do decide to give chase, but it's not a foregone conclusion that they'd revoke you immediately. If that were the case, we'd all be living under One Government by now. Thank Heavens for small miracles.

But, what if your passport is revoked? How would you travel to other countries?

That depends. Assuming you have a valid one, it'll be up to any country you visit that complies with the revocation. If they do, you won't be able to visit that country until you get a new one. Fortunately this doesn't apply to the entire world (yet).

From the US State Department Website at travel.state.gov:

A federal or state law enforcement agency may request the denial of a passport on several regulatory grounds under 22 CFR 51.70 and 51.72. The principal law enforcement reasons for passport denial are a federal warrant of arrest, a federal or state criminal court order, a condition of parole or probation forbidding departure from the United States (or the jurisdiction of the court), or a request for extradition. The HHS child support database and the Marshals Service WIN database are checked automatically for entitlement to a passport. Denial or revocation of a passport does not prevent the use of outstanding valid passports.

If any one country allows someone to fly on that country's own airline, they can without even having any passport at all - so long as the destination country agrees. That's right, you don't even need a passport if it's been stolen while you were in Bangkok or wherever. As it can take days for a new one to arrive, you can go to the consulate and get them to tell the right people, "It's OK, this person isn't Edward Snowden, so he's good to go."

Only it's somewhat rare this happens, which is reason enough to ensure you've got a Plan B and Plan C and so on before you start running.

Mistake 3: Losing Face

Showing your face, even in a public setting outside your own country, can kill your anonymity quicker than a lightning strike right down your spine. This nail in the coffin has a two-pronged effect: The first being that old-fashioned virtue we call honesty. With it, Snowden could address the American public without there being any doubt to the validity of his identity. If he'd stayed anonymous, he'd have always struggled with proving who he was and that his words rung true. We all exhibit various flavors of skepticism, after all.

The second effect is that the FBI now knew his face. Eventually, the NSA would've nailed him even if he hadn't gone public, but it might have given him more time since Snowden's appeal could very well have dragged out any extradition request.

Takeaway lesson: Don't flee to a country that will do you more harm than the country you are fleeing *from*. While we see Edward living a somewhat normal, if modest life in that sprawling ex-Soviet country, it could mean that life may be short lived. When the dust settles, and the comedian skits cease, and we no longer hear of Snowden or WikiLeaks, we may just miss an incident where Putin decides to be a little more forceful in gaining access to that vault of secrets between Edward's ears. Don't let that be you. Know your destination country inside and out.

Defeating Facial Recognition Technology

As much as I like Spiderman, I know I can't vanish around the corner of a building 6 floors up using nothing but my webby finger. And I'm not Quicksilver, either, much as I'd love to be. He can run 200 mph and push bullets around like Skittles. Better still is that both of the above men have what I call 'enhanced' gut-checking ability. Quicksilver for instance, knew that Wolverine and Beast were up to no good as soon as they drove up to his mother's house. He thought they were cops. They weren't. But that didn't stop him from checking their IDs at the speed of light.

For us, staying invisible also requires a gut check; that rare ability to listen to your gut when it tells you you're walking into a danger zone.

Disappearing in cities is harder than it looks. That's because 2015 is a very different urban beast than it was in the year 2000. Street cams are everywhere. So how do we deal with them if we need to go off the grid for a while?

Simple. We plan in advance.

I'm sure you don't care for the government using facial-scan technology, and to be honest neither do I. I don't care for being monitored for my 'carbon footprints' nor the RIAA checking to hear if I'm whistling a copyrighted tune out of my backside. With all the cams everywhere, it's hard not visiting a medieval sword shop and taking Gimli's double-bladed axe to every one of the blasted things.

That'd be a very long hack, indeed, but it'd be playing whack-a-mole. Three new ones would appear for every one I destroyed. And resorting to violence only leads to the slammer, anyway.

That said, let's go over what those Orwellian things can do and what they can't.

First of all, facial recognition isn't like the sort you see on Star Trek episodes, nor is it a perfect way to spot a kidnapper. There's good sides and bad sides to it. The good news is that there are flaws that can be exploited. When you hear about facial recognition technology like that used by social networks, what they really refer to is the techniques used to identify a photo, or a moving face in a reel of film.

The algorithms target spacial differences and anomalies along your face: how far the chin protrudes for example, or how far the eyes are apart and even the biometrics of the ears, and so forth. Does she have Asian features? How about Russian cheekbones and nose? Indonesian lips? There are almost a hundred nodes along a human face for an algorithm to work with. That doesn't sound so good to someone wanting to disappear.

The worst part is that it only takes twenty or so nodes relative to a man or woman's face to be identified. If a satellite can identify a person's brand of shoe from low orbit, you can imagine how easy it'd be to size up a person's face and match that with a database.

But there's a silver lining. Even mathematical algorithms can be tricked. Take Google, for example. Google spends billions on its algorithms every year, and much less on its programmers, which coincidentally happen to be some of the best on Earth. Yet it's often simple, unexpected techniques that blackhat marketers use to fool Google into thinking data is relevant and should be ranked on first page of search results... when it really doesn't. A false positive, to say. Google coders adapt the code, but the blackhat marketers catch on because word spreads around the hive mind quickly in blackhat forums.

As we saw with student loans, there are shady and not so shady ways of dealing with them. Here are the quasi-legal not-too-shady ways:

1.) Look At Your Feet

Alex Kilpatrick is a facial-recognition expert and research leader at the TIS (Tactical Info Systems) company in Texas. He did an interview for the BBC where he talked about simple ways to defeat these facial recognition systems, one of which was to look at your feet as you walk. This obscures your identity in ways the cameras can't account for. And yes, you guessed right if you said the homeless have the advantage here.

Way back before surveillance cams flooded the Louisiana educational system, I studied at Loyola University in New Orleans, right across the street from Audubon Park. It was hard as acorns some days. The squirrels ate better than I did. To alleviate this, I donated plasma. Gallons of the stuff.

Donating my own plasma (despite my fear of needles and math) kept my belly full during the few hard months that I had to wait for my student loan check to arrive. I know, I know. Poor baby, right?

Only I wasn't alone. Lots of students did this to survive. Selling plasma back then was a lot safer than selling drugs. There were a few days when I feared passing out for tricking the phlebotomist into donating more than I should've. I passed out more than once on campus. I even passed out in the plasma center after staring at the blood-red Kool-Aid dispenser for a little too long. I went down hard and bashed my lip on the countertop just as they were sliding my daily $20 across to me. Talk about blood money.

The other thing I dreaded back then, other than math and needles, were the belching RTA buses. They belched smog everywhere and spurt oil like some lumbering brontosaurus marking it's territory around town. A squirt here, a dump there. The buses stunk, too. They were also very overcrowded, and the inside always smelled worse than the outside. Think Taun-Tauns from the Empire Strikes Back, only in Manila-like heat.

The worst part though, was that it'd take me two hours to get someplace that'd only take ten minutes by car. I figured other students in rival cities had it just as bad.

Then there was the bummy smell. Bums who rode with splayed legs across the aisle like some sleeping wino. They threw trash everywhere. They carried rotten fruit to the back, drawing flies. And heaven help you if you were on board at 3pm when the fifth graders boarded. It was like being invaded. Thousands of uniformed gremlins stormed to the back, cussing like rabid gremlins finally free of some tyrant's regime in the sewers.

Saturdays were a little better. Less kids then, but fewer buses, especially along the lakefront area where the University of New Orleans sat. On one weekend, I walked several long and littered blocks or so down Canal Street, aka Bum Central. It was an educational walk, and I recall bringing along my abnormal psych book to kill time. Lord knows why. When I got off and started walking with that beast of a book in hand, I'd occasionally look up to notice how similar the bourbon drunk's style of walking was to the wino's. You've seen the style no doubt.

A bum walks with his head down over a long beard, shot glass of bourbon in one hand and Nighttrain in the other, only they have that swagger like they're walking on a rusty bridge over the Mississippi. After a good while, I began to see that they knew how to blend in. The entire street had several theaters and I'd see them hawk and hork and spit and panhandle the rich tourists that stepped off the streetcars. A few even wore sunglasses, hoodie and sweatpants, but they all seemed to grow out their beards to biblical lengths. I took it all in like a scientist studying some lost pygmy tribe.

Sunglasses Don't Work

I thought at the time that perhaps a few of those bums wanted to be trendy bums. But the problem with wearing shades in order to fool surveillance cams, is that the algorithm will ignore that section of your face and focus more intensely on other parts of it. In fact, I'd say judging from the research done by the Chinese on facial recognition systems, it doesn't matter how big the glasses are, either.

Obnoxious Clothing Works

If you've got a few articles of clothing with pictures of other people's faces on it, that'll disrupt the algorithm in the same way billboards disrupt Google Earth's Street View algorithm, the same that smears real people's faces on the street for privacy reasons.

Clothing like this:

Or this:

You don't necessarily need to go with a "face shirt" either, and the image below is probably a stretch:

Helmets

A beard and hat disguise is better than wearing a helmet for too long. A friend of mine remarked that he wears a full face helmet whenever he rides his motorcycle. Keeps the bugs out of his hair, he says. Only when he tries to pump gasoline while wearing it, the gas attendant won't turn on the pumps until he takes it *off*.

Well, no wet-behind-the-ears teenager is going to tell him what to do, so off he goes to another gas station. An Exxon this time. Only the end result is the same. He found out that the owners of these gas stations like to have a biker's face on the camera in case the police come by asking about a kidnapped child.

IR LEDs

Remember that what facial recognition systems zero-in on are *relative triangles*, like the tip of your nose to the bottom of your chin, and over to your ears, or from your chin to your forehead and over to your eyes. You're unique in this way just as your fingerprints are unique. No two people are the same.

But an IR LED laser disrupts this nicely. We discussed laser pointers disrupting instruments on jets. Well, the same principle applies here, and I predict this'll find its way into our clothing styles in the coming years whether we like it or not, depending on how invasive Big Brother's systems evolve.

The downside is that it doesn't work unless *everyone* is doing it, since by using this you'll clearly stand out on a monitor. Some celebrities used to wear these to discourage the paparazzi whenever they'd go out. It was set off by a camera flash and the results were not quite what they'd hoped.

Then again, the antivirus company AVG (now.avg.com) is reportedly working on so-called "invisibility glasses" that thwart facial software altogether. It uses LEDs that move around the eyes and nose, which distort any images the system takes for the purpose of recognizing you.

College Dorms

A dorm is the worst possible place for privacy. At Loyola University, during my junior year, I as well as every other resident of the Cabra Hall residence building had to show our IDs to the desk attendant. Every time.

Now, I know there's nothing unusual about that. It is, after all, a somewhat high crime area and they only want to check the validity of their residents, right? Only it never seemed to matter that we'd spoken to the desk attendant a thousand times that day or even that we were related to her. Neither did it matter if we swiped the card without an error and had come through not an hour prior.

Every single time we walked through the front double-steel doors to that fortress of doom, we got the "Papers please!" spiel. Every single time.

It wasn't long before the graduate student sitting behind the dusty counter caught me on a bad day, and after a hard rain and a failed calculus test, I refused. Flat out refused. It felt a little ham fisted, but it was strangely relieving. Like I'd had a gigantic weight lifted off my shoulders. Maybe I'd just needed to vent. Who knows, but I never expected the response I got.

She chewed me out something fierce. Like I'd just shot a litter of cheetah cubs or something. For a moment I considered stabbing my finger into her face and yelling how ridiculous this new so called security practice was, since the on-campus crime rate hadn't budged an inch all semester.

But no, that'd just give her and others above her the attention they craved, I figured, so I just walked right by her as though I'd swallowed an invisibility potion.

She didn't like that stunt either, and the next time I came around at dinnertime, about 7 o'clock in the evening after a heavy downpour, she lashed out at me with a few insults she'd brewed up in my absence. Insults probably brewed in some black cauldron that was hidden somewhere in the back, out of the public's view.

I got pretty steamed and fired back.

I frisbeed my ID at her like that feral kid did with his makeshift boomerang in The Road Warrior; so fast I thought it'd put her eye out. It struck her forehead dead center before tumbling away, over her desk and down her arm and into her bookbag. I froze.

I'd meant to miss her. Skim the attitude-dropping cat's hairline. Only I ended up hitting her dead center.

Soon, I'd be hanged or flogged in the rain or tied to the front of an RTA bus and paraded around the Ninth Ward with some racist screed scrawled across my chest. I just knew this wouldn't be the end of it.

Next thing I knew I was shuffled into the resident manager's office to justify my terrorist-like actions. With the firestorm that ensued, you'd think I'd crashed a drone into a football blimp. After he simmered down, I went to excuse myself after I'd issued every lawyered-up apology I could think of. He sighed long and loud and whistled through his nose as he stared down at me - very much like black dragon, now that I think about it. And those nostrils. Sweet Jesus it was like looking into the barrel of a shotgun.

I wanted out and fast.

So I stood up to shake his hand... and saw the Mac display behind him. There, in Matrix-green, were my midterm grades for all the world to see as naked as a newborn baby. He noticed my shock, looked over his shoulder and huffed. He sat down hard. Then he went down each course, mashing a finger next to each D and C-, making snide remarks about unfit I was to be in such a fine, safe ivory institution. He then snapped that if I didn't value the surveillance for my own safety, then maybe I should go sleep with the bums out near the French Quarter, or take a job as a horse n' buggy tour guide. Or stick my head in a croc's mouth out at the Swamp Tours place.

I was more pissed at the bummy threat. He actually threatened to introduce me to a few of the hard case bums that'd given him some trouble. Well, I told him I didn't need any introductions as I'd already met an army of them over the last year. I wanted to tell him off further, but I held my tongue. I started to leave when he criticized my upbringing. Even brought my mother into it.

I bit my lip so hard it bled. "Jeuus Chryss," I said, and then proceeded to take back every apology. I catapulted a few fiery insults of my own, mostly ones I'd heard on the bus ride over. Gremlin-approved insults (though a bit lispy).

I almost enjoyed sitting out a semester.

Going To Extremes

Someday your troubles may just drive you to do something drastic. Like sail halfway across the world to some tropical paradise where you can bury your troubles right next to where your dog Rip buries his bones - in a hole as deep and wet and as dark as Texas crude.

If I had a choice on where to disappear, I'd pick Scaramanga's island hideout. If you've ever seen The Man with the Golden Gun, you'd know it matches the blue splendor of Bora Bora and even Boracay. And it's a helluva lot cheaper.

Khow-Ping-Kan, or 'James Bond Isle' as it's called, offers a fantastic place for meditation. That's the best reason to go. The other reason only enhances the first reason: a chain of limestone pillars covered in jungle vines dot the islands in a way that brings your thoughts alive.

The place was Paradise back when Bond filmed there. Unspoiled and tranquil and worry free. Now it's a hive filled with Phuket tourists, where everyone wears rainbow outfits and flip-floppy clown shoes like they just stepped off the bus to Tijuana with Krusty the Clown.

But when the crowds leave, and you're out there all alone and hear the waves and smell the fish and taste the saltiness of the water, you realize a simple truth. You realize that each man needs an escape. His own domain. A study for deep reflection. Prayer. A sanctuary. It soon dawns on you that this is an impossibility for everyone. So you begin to meditate on how to get your own.

I used to laugh at people who meditated. It reminded me of Bette Midler or some rich diva meditating in Beverly Hills with a yapping pink-dyed poodle. Only now, I'm the one meditating.

What do I meditate about? Everything exotic you can dream up.

In the old days it was just the opposite. Back then it was things I couldn't control. Things like student loans, credit cards, car problems, taxes, girlfriend drama, parental drama, tuition hikes, traffic, interest, hurricanes in New Orleans, blizzards in Canada, lightning strikes in the rain and tornadoes in Texas... none of which I had any control over.

The one thing I could control, was my *response* to each and every one of those things - which was to leave them behind.

It turned out to be a life-changing experience. I learned, for example, that pictures in a glossy travel brochure can't convey what 110 degrees feels like on your back, and that you felt safer feeding whale sharks.

Nor can that same brochure relay the kind of terror that comes with feeling a shark's sandpaper fin scrape your leg as you surf. And it cannot give you the feel of a waif filching your wallet. If any of the above are deal killers for you, think twice about moving to say, Phukit, or anywhere else unless you tackle those head on. A week-long vacation is one thing, but to live in Thailand or China or Philippines brings it's own set of unique challenges. If you've a fear of water, heights, closed-in spaces or spiders, be prepared to adjust.

I never allowed any of those things stop me, and they shouldn't stop you either. We get one ride around this crazy carousel called life, and it'll be the things you never did and the risks you never took that'll give you regret in your old age.

It sounds exaggerated. Only it isn't. You may be thinking that your problems aren't bad enough to warrant that kind of migration. Too risky. And too hot. It's too crowded, too, and you've no intention of leaving the safety of your own country. You'll stand out like a hillbilly's busted toe on Facebook and you'll never see your kids again.

To that I say bull.

You could travel for any number of reasons, and they're probably all justified. Perhaps not to everyone, but then everyone doesn't know how traumatic your life is. Only you and the Almighty do. You may find that you just need to get away to an exotic place to heal. Recharge. That's near impossible to do if Betsy from SallieMae loans is constantly harassing your family every hour on the hour, and with Uncle Frick threatening to kick you to the curb if they don't stop, well, that's a ticking time bomb that'll blow up in your face sooner or later.

And it's a lousy way to heal.

Worrying can kill you in ways that'd make the grim reaper blush. Ulcers. Diabetes. Cancer. Worry fuels each and every one of these conditions, and each day is a knock on the grim reaper's front door if you don't take action. There's no reason TransRecovery Collections needs to accelerate it by giving you a heart attack. So you just tell that redheaded bat that you're saving for a Russian-made suitcase nuke and not to call you anymore.

That said, there's something you need to know about exotic places should you decide to make a run for it: Your problems follow you like a stray puppy.

And I don't mean just your *financial* problems. Over there, your student loans won't mean jack. We both know that. It's the *personal issues*. Hardwired emotional circuitry like anger. Jealousy. Alcoholism. Drag racing. Base jumping. Cat hoarding. Skydiving naked. Whatever your ethic, whatever your spiritual weakness, whatever your fix, it won't magically change when you leave the West, so don't hightail it to Coron Island to scuba dive in a bombed out WWII sub thinking your old habits won't follow.

With that said, let's look at some destinations that may give you some time to heal - without distraction.

Philippines

It wasn't the $1400 sticker shock of the plane ticket to
Philippines that nearly had me in tears, or even the 18 hour
flight. It was the *sweltering* heat. I sweat like I'd been spit
roasted by one of those fire-twirlers in Bora Bora. I
remember folding my arms behind my head on my hotel
bed and contemplating running back home. It was an alien
planet to me. Though New Orleans was no piece of cake
by far, I knew that even our July heat was nothing to
Manila's mercurial air. Not to mention the smog and
roosters everywhere. I began to think a few only went to
Mass to escape the heat. Who could blame them?

Heat aside, I found that life slows to a crawl in Cebu and
Manila, but relationships run cheetah speed. Walk around
a Cebu market and you'll see for yourself. As long as you
don't resemble an ogre, you'll be shocked at how forward
and affectionate Filipinas can be to western men. Me
included.

I was wholly unprepared for this strange new world. When
I gathered enough courage to scout around town, dodging
stray cats and wandering roosters, I managed a few
conversations. My 'Nice Guy' persona was assaulted. It
was as if I'd turned into Rex Nebular, naive space
adventurer newly stranded on a planet of attention-starved
Amazon women - with me being the only guy available.
Turns out, I was the only *white guy* available. Big
difference, since a lot of their favorite stars have milky

white skin - a trait they hope to instill in their offspring. I didn't know this at the time.

Soon came the date requests. They didn't seem to understand the words 'no, not interested.' In hindsight, I doubt they could. It'd have been like turning down a backstage pass with a rock star. And believe me I'm no rock star. But neither am I one of those two old farts from the Muppets. To this effect, a friend commented on this anomaly, saying that it's like being a rock star at a concert nobody attends. I think he was referring to the void of Western men here.

I eventually gave in to a few requests. The lessons I learned, I learned the hard way.

The hardest lesson was that things progress quickly in SE Asia. By the fourth date, I sensed I was being proposed to. I politely declined. I had to. The date ended and I walked back at my hotel thinking it another anomaly. Something was off though. Then that feeling of 'being off' grew worse, since the next date produced the same effect. And the next. And the next. And all in under a two month time frame. It was outrageous. Were they all golddiggers? I wondered. It seemed to fly right over their heads when I explained that it usually took a year, minimum, back in the states before anything like marriage was discussed. Things move fast here, they said.

Then I learned how to tell the good girls from the bad. Usually, a good way to tell is if she wants you to meet the parents. Any girl worth dating will want to do this as soon as possible. After which, you're hooked. From that point forward you'll be on a tight leash. She won't let you out of her sight because she knows the risk of losing you to another girl is quite powerful.

Even a stroll through the SM Mall will all but guarantee you'll have massive numbers of women approach you. It's no exaggeration. Expats who live there may scoff, but that's because they're used to it. The novelty wears off after a few months. But if you are in Davao, Cebu, Dumaguete, or pretty much anywhere except Manila and Zamboanga, this is a fact of life. Filipinas love foreigners. A few love their money, but many simply want to be loved and someone to love in return.

When this happened to me, I recalled something a friend had mentioned about his trip to Tokyo. So-called 'Gaijin' lovers, or foreigner lovers - Japanese men and women who'd hit you up on the subway with a metric-ton of questions, and all for just being a foreigner. A celebrity foreigner, like Ryan Gosling for example. Only in the Philippines, the celebrity factor's a few notches higher than in Japan. When this happens in Tokyo, it feels patronizing and anything but romantic. In the Philippines, it's almost *always* romantic. Filipinas have this strange thing they do with their eyebrows that makes it seem like they're flirting 100% of the time. Call it a blessing in disguise?

But like with most blessings, it seems that in this rainy country of jeepneys and fishing boats, the blessings all have a catch. All of this unexpected attention, where the sweet, endearing Filipinas take lovely pictures of you eating by yourself at the mall and come up to you to say,

'You're too handsome to be eating by yourself, may I join you?" comes at a rather high cost.

That cost is your anonymity.

Once the cat is out of the bag, getting her back is like turning water into wine, and you know how cats just *love* water.

The reason anonymity is difficult in the Philippines is not only because of the rock star effect you'll give off, but because it's one of the most networked countries in the world. And I don't mean the internet, either. Sure, they'll post your picture they took of you to every social media outlet in the universe, but they'll tell everyone they know from the southern tip of Zamboanga to the northern shanties of Manila about you... in person.

"He's so *guapo!* (handsome)."

"How white his skin is! Bet his kids look like angels!"

"I wonder what position he likes..." (I heard a girl mumble this as I walked by)

Cousins, stepbrothers and their stepfather's golf partner's brother-in-laws, the whole lot of them will shred your privacy to bits. All of them. I was taken aback by the inter-connectedness of the Philippines, so much that it seemed everyone had as many relatives as Jawas did on Tatooine. Networks weren't just limited to online outlets, but face to face interactions. They were everywhere. In the malls. In the parks. In the unused baseball fields. Along the beach and boat marinas. Small groups. Big groups. They love to gather and gossip and talk and forge friendships the way we do on the Fourth of July. You can see how this might be a problem if you value privacy.

If you really like a girl but then later have coffee with a different girl, your main girl *will* find out about it. There are Facebook groups that out cheaters, nevermind that a few girls mark their territory. A hair barret behind the toilet, for example. Or a few hairs sticking out of your Playstation 4 or gamepad. It's a signal to a rival girl that you're taken. So strong is the hyper-networked culture in the Philippines, that it's like the nerves of a sperm whale. The tail knows what the head is doing.

That's the good and the bad of the Philippines. Now for the ugly. Here it is:

Filipino men, in particular, are notoriously jealous, sometimes to the point of violence. Women may run what's called 'Tampo' on you, where they clam up for hours or days if you've upset them. But the men can be downright deadly if you steal their girl.

If you manage to find yourself getting threats by the 'other guy', don't brush them off. Take each threat seriously. They won't start a fistfight with you like they do in Texas or Alberta. They'll likely use a .22 pistol to settle the score, and on a day when you least expect it. My advice is to choose someone else.

The reason is this: if you're fighting with a Pinoy, it can escalate just as quickly as the romantic interactions with a filipina can. It just may escalate into a High Noon situation. Then you've got a major problem on your hands.

It's odd that fist fights don't settle things here like they sometimes do in the states. The Wild West mentality is rampant here. You splash Wyatt Earp's face with a shot of bourbon whiskey in his own saloon, where every gal is watching, what do you think is going to happen? That's how it is here when two men want the same woman.

It could be something sent privately, like the kind my friend received for hitting on an 18 year old Cebuana. I remember the text he shared with me.

'That my girl you hit on. You stay away! No trouble! Or I break a bottle and cut your ass!'

Sounds juvenile. Most guys back home would blow this off. Well, some maybe.

Your average 20 year old surfer tourist on summer break here sometimes thinks he can shoot like Doc Holliday in a thunderstorm while riding a horse sideways. It's frustrating to watch. Like a slow-motion showing of the Evil Dead.

After a few Red Horse beers, he smarts off like a stubborn mule that doesn't want to budge. He shoots back to that Pinoy that he can date whom he pleases, where he pleases, and when he pleases, consequences be damned. And if that Pinoy wants a fight? Well then he can just bring it right on come day or night.

Another American tried this not too long ago. He was assassinated over a dispute with the other fellow, who claimed he was stealing his girl. The man walked right up to him in broad daylight not two days later and put two slugs in the man's head just as he got off his motorcycle. This was in a crowded area, too, and the poor sap never saw it coming. Judas Iscariot could not have backstabbed a person better.

The assassin, as justice would have it, was sentenced to prison for decades, and all over a girl that wasn't that different than any of the other millions in the Philippines. At trial the judge asked him if he regretted his decision.

"Sure do. I regret a lot sir," he said. "I regret I'm not gonna see my wife and two children again. I regret that part."

There are other incidents. Usually they're started over money or property. One Pinoy who worked security for an American businessman ended up getting fired. Everyone I've spoken with agrees that he deserved to get fired. The man was always late. He'd insult the customers. He'd drink on the job. Fart as loud as he could. A real slimeball who engaged cockfighting but was a sore loser and almost always sought revenge. So finally one day the boss said, "You know what? I deserve better than this. You're fired."

The next day that Pinoy came in and shot the man dead, point-blank. And all over a lousy security guard job.

Other stories abound. One I dread involves the tale of a Marine who took what he perceived (in a drunken state) to be the best looking supermodel in the entire Southeast

Asian continent. She was stunning, at least at the bar. Long legs, so taller than most Pinays who're no more than 5'2, and with a nice personality and good intelligence. So what went wrong?

Well little did he know that the 'girl' he escorted back to his apartment... wasn't. It was a tranny.

When the ball dropped, he strangled that guy to death and was soon arrested for murder. He's now looking at twenty to life in a Philippine prison, and all for little more than a smack to the ego. He could've thrown him outside and no one would've been the wiser.

As a westerner from America, Canada or the UK, there are two hundred Filipinas in line to date you, with many being far prettier, sweeter and eager to please you and far less trouble than what the present girl is giving you back home in the Land of the Free. Life is short enough as it is. If you're wondering what you could possibly say to diffuse that Pinoy time bomb from going off, this is what I would've texted back:

"Hey friend, sorry for the confusion. Didn't mean to interfere. Her and I aren't serious. Plenty of girls to pick from so you'll get no trouble from me. Ciao --"

It sounds short and submissive, like something Deputy Fife might say. And it is. Maybe that's not you at all. Maybe you're the type who finishes bar brawls.

Listen friend, I've suffered enough broken noses and busted teeth to tell you that you'll save yourself a world of headache and prison time if you abide by something Aristotle said: "It's an act of superiority to confer a kindness to someone, but a mark of inferiority to receive it."

Pinays

Pinay /'piːnaɪ/ is a colloquial term for Filipina, the feminine form of Pinoy. Pinoy was used for self-identification by the first wave of Filipinos going to the continental United States before World War II and has been used both in a pejorative sense as well as a term of endearment similar to Chicano.

That's the technical definition.

I'm not sure if it's viewed as derogatory by some of them, but I've never met a Filipina that was offended by it. Maybe in America, but certainly not in Philippines as I've come to know it.

One related word that was surprisingly hard to find was 'Tampo'. That's probably because it's more of a general attitude than a noun like Filipina. I couldn't find it at the Webster site, nor at Wikipedia or anywhere else. Funny, I've always felt that the word Pinay and Tampo should be grouped together like peas and carrots, since 90% of the Filipinas I've met over the years practice it right along with Mass attendance on Sundays.

So now that I've piqued your interest, here's what it means: Tampo is Filipina lingo meaning 'to give you the cold shoulder'. The silent treatment. It's something a Pinay does to signal you've messed up somewhere along the way. By the time you recognize it, your head'll spin trying to remember where you mucked it all up because a lot of them stew for a good while before hitting the eject button. By that time, you're in a downward spiral, in flames. And it almost always happens when you least expect it. In my case, on vacation in a variety of places:

- On the way to the hotel in Cebu.

- On the beach in Palawan.

- At the bar, when I got a little too Guy Smiley with the pretty bartender.

- When I got a panoramic view of some unexpected cleavage, courtesy of a bargirl; one eager beaver who was all too accidental in dropping things a little close to our table.

- Forgetting the flip-flops *and* forgetting to remind her to bring the tampon box for the beach trip.

A friend of mine complained how immature it seemed as he spent a weekend in Davao. He told me that as far as he knew, everything went fine from the time they stepped out of the taxi until their arrival at the beach. It was only *after* they entered the lush, flowery room that she initiated 'tampo'. Nothing could snap her out of that vampiric state. It was like trying to coax a gargoyle statue to life.

But he persisted.

"Sugar, do you want to take a shower before heading out to the beach?"

Dead air.

"You want a nice back rub? I bet your nerves are flaring after that nasty traffic."

He might as well have asked a vampire muppet. This even lasted half the day!

My approach to resolving this is very different than my friend's tactic. I've found that 'lambing' (kissing ass) does little to disarm that bomb since you're essentially rewarding that type of behavior. Doing so guarantees a repeat performance.

I don't know about you, but one big 'boom' is enough for me. What works is to lay the ground rules from the very beginning. State how 'tampo' is a deal breaker for you, and that any girl who employs this shady tactic will be shown the door. It's an issue of mistrust, after all. If she doesn't trust your reaction enough to tell you what's wrong, then she's not ready to commit to you. She's not *mature* enough for a relationship. Once you've picked up a cat who doesn't want a bath by the scruff of it's neck, she usually gets the point.

Employment in The Philippines

Easy living is cheap in the Philippines. You can live in a native-style hut near Puerto Galera for about a hundred bucks, or pay two to three grand for a higher-end place near the beach in Cebu. In fact you may be dreaming up a nice working vacation of sorts. Grab your backpack, fly over and fund a week's worth of margaritas and coral reefs in Boracay, with a part-time gig in a call center. There's tons of them after all and honestly, how hard can it be to secure something like that?

Well I'll tell you. It's *brutally* hard if you're used to western wages.

Even a full-time gig working in a call center will pay *maybe* $400 dollars a month, or about 10-20,000 pesos. Entire families live on that, and most Filipinos work long hours on their feet at SM Mall, without breaks. Twelve hour shifts are the norm and whenever they get a polite and well-dressed Noir-smelling westerner hitting on them on a sour day, when their face feels like its turning into a monochrome statue and their legs are aching, they light up bigger than the Christmas tree in Times Square. And you would too, believe me.

Many are college educated and many even have Master's degrees in business. To be honest, your best bet is to work off your laptop, preferably near the water. Many expats do and live like a king in Southeast Asia. There's plenty of ways to make money online, but the biggest paychecks I've seen come from two areas: Writing, and Marketing. Writers come in all flavors as you know, so you have to ask yourself what kind of writer you are or want to become.

Travel writer? Editor? Children's book author? Or maybe you like the business side of writing, also known as copywriting.

Copywriters are writers who write sales copy and book blurbs and ad slogans on Odesk and eLance and Fiverr. It takes months of daily practice to write good sales copy. You also have to build a nice portfolio website and client base if you want to live on it. The website is so you can show your ad copy and any book blurbs you sold to fiction writers over at Fiverr.

Not having any website is the number one killer of every amateur writer I've ever met. A lot of them will procrastinate. They think it's just all too hard or a waste of time or that they need ten grand to hire a competent coder. Nope, nothing of the sort. Go to Fiverr and you'll see tons of offers for dirt cheap.

Then you have the Amazon writers. Some are fiction novelists and others enjoy writing non-fiction. They upload their books everywhere: Amazon. Apple. Google Books. Smashwords. And they do it all without a traditional publisher. They're *self*-publishers and get paid 70% royalty in most places. That goes far in the Philippines.

I'm a self-publisher, and it took me more than a year before I was making half a grand, but I was thrilled to get it because I was doing what I loved, and that half a grand per month went light years farther in Philippines than it did in Canada or New Orleans. The only roadblock is yourself.

If on the other hand you're *not* a writer, look into turning a hobby into a business. Dive shops are one idea, but they require ten grand and extensive knowledge of a lot of different things like scuba gear, sharks, and anti-venom for the times when someone will touch a poisonous plant and threaten to sue you. This happens often, I'm told.

All of the above will give you far less headaches than working in a Filipino call center, and for a fraction of the time required.

Property Titles

Thinking about opening up a posh hotel in the Philippines? Maybe kickstart a small casino with a pool and a great fiery sunset view of the ocean with roulette tables spinning in the background? It makes for a great scene doesn't it? Like something out of Casino Royale.

But beware... Do your research **first** before anything else.

Before marketing. Before building. Before even scouting for a nice, cozy spot on the white sandy beach.

There are a few abandoned sites that looked to be great casinos back in the day, that now are ghost towns. In almost every case I researched, the investor neglected to do his due diligence on licensing; titles, gambling licenses, land permits and the sort. A few now sit deserted in a canopy of ferns and sand and white shells that no child collects. Walking in one of these ghostly places is like walking through Jurassic Park *after* everyone had fled or'd been eaten by velociraptors.

Don't let the same happen to you. You'll be eaten alive by regulators if you don't heed this simple advice, so spend a month or hire an investigator to look into it, and triple-check everything.

Costs

Alright, alright, but what does it cost to live there?

A lot less than it does to startup a casino.

The Jun n' Dell Apartment Complex in Davao was cheap for me, at $400 per month. And that came with plenty of amenities, just about everything I needed: Cable. Internet. Power. Water.

The biggest bonus, however, was that I seemed more stable to the locals since I wasn't renting a motel room. Do that and people'll think you're not worth investing the time in because, well, Pinays and Pinoys tend to be more hesitant to get to know a tourist than a local. If you're in the local Motel-6, anyone you talk to will know you're not staying for the long haul. If you lie about it, they'll find out. Luckily, places like Jun N' Dell rent by the month, and since they is no lease, that's less sweat off your back. This is the better option since you want as many allies as you can get no matter what part of the Philippines you're in.

Davao is ultra cheap for most necessities, but at the same time is comfortable. Comfortable, though, or just 'good enough' often isn't quite comfortable enough if you're a business traveler who needs to disappear for a while *and* who wants top notch accommodations. For that kind of experience, I'd recommend the Marco Polo hotel over Jun n' Dell. You'll pay a lot more, but reap ten times the benefits.

Here's a rundown on what you'd spend for a month in Davao, which would of course be more in a place like Manila or Cebu or Boracay since those are the popular tourist destinations. But this should give you an idea of what to expect.

Rent Per Month

Apartment (1 bedroom) in City Centre	$180.33
Apartment (1 bedroom) Outside of Centre	$111.79

Apartment (3 bedrooms) in City Centre $278.90
Apartment (3 bedrooms) Outside of Centre $213.63

Utilities

Basic (Electricity, Heating, Water, Garbage) for a 900 sq ft Apt $46.83
1 min. of Prepaid Mobile Tariff Local (No Plan) $0.16
Internet (10 Mbps, Unlimited Data, Cable/ADSL) $37.74

Restaurants

Meal, Inexpensive Restaurant $1.86
Meal for 2, Mid-range Restaurant, Three-course $11.00
McMeal at McDonalds (or Equivalent Combo Meal) $2.08
Domestic Beer $0.95
Imported Beer $2.20

Sports And Leisure

Fitness Club, Monthly Fee for 1 Adult $24.37
Tennis Court Rent (1 Hour on Weekend) $3.30
Cinema, 1 Seat $2.86

Clothing And Shoes
1 Pair of Jeans (Levis 501) $36.28
1 Summer Dress in a Chain Store (Zara, H&M) $28.15
1 Pair of Nike Running Shoes (Mid-Range) $67.54
1 Pair of Men Leather Business Shoes $50.58

Salary

Average Monthly Disposable Salary (After Tax)
   $280.38

(Source: Numbeo.com)

Visas

Getting a tourist visa in the Philippines couldn't be easier.

The trip though, can be nightmarishly long. The flight drags on and on like a Gone with the Wind marathon. Twenty hours by my watch, and you may just be able to watch it entirely on the way over without falling asleep. I almost made it.

Once you arrive in Manila, you can head on over to the Immigration office (across the street from an old Spanish fort and a Starbucks), where they'll stamp your passport for a 21 day stay automatically. It's that easy. After that, you can extend it for another 38 days at any Immigration office. If you want to stay even longer, you can extend it every 2 months for up to 16 months *without leaving the country*. So you can stay in the country for two years on nothing but a tourist visa.

However, there's a snag many new expats encounter: Round-trip plane tickets.

Many airlines won't let you board the plane if you haven't bought a return flight. This double-vision has more to do with the airlines than it does with the Philippines. They don't want you crying to them for a free plane trip home should you happen to be robbed of everything you hold dear. This happens frequently.

They've been burned in the past because people *who don't plan in advance* do dumb things like carry around $1000 in cash while they cruise around Manila in a jeepney. These people can be dangerous. They're often gluttons for punishment. Repeat offenders. Sometimes I wonder if they paint the red target on their backs themselves.

Years ago some British and American tourists returned to the Philippines *even after* the airlines graciously paid their way home... only to be robbed *again*. So the business-savvy airlines enacted this rule of not letting anyone aboard who doesn't have a return flight in hand. Sort of like Ms. Needles the morbid math teacher punishing the entire class when no one fesses up to the wet sock full of tacks put on her chair.

A friend relayed how, when he boarded a plane from LAX to Manila, they repeatedly said that he needed an *onward* ticket. He told them his friend already bought one, but that he couldn't access it for them at that moment. They didn't buy it. After haggling for what seemed an eternity, he finally met with a manager who made him sign a letter stating that if he were to be denied entry into the Philippines, the airline would refuse to pay for a return ticket to LAX. Now, this was in the States - long before he got anywhere near Manila.

But there's a way around it. Two actually, one of which is a bit shady.

First, don't purchase a return ticket out of the Philippines. Instead, go to Expedia, create an account, save a planned itinerary from say Manila to Bangkok, and then email it to yourself. Cut and paste it into a Word document but remove the spot where it says, "NOT BOOKED YET" and replace with "CONFIRMED". Done. You now have a return ticket with your name and flight number.

The non-shady way is to book an onward flight to some cheap China city close to the border, most of which are cheap. Like less than a $100 cheap. Then cancel that flight when you arrive in Manila. A lot of expats do this and save themselves a tons of headaches and frustration.

Embassies

It's been said that poor decisions and bad luck are often contingencies of most horror films. And I'd agree, especially where getting stranded is concerned. There's nothing better than a good horror film where we can root for some poor underdog whose been stranded for eons. It's easier to root from a plush sofa. You've probably seen a few of my favorites:

The Thing. The Fog. The Walking Dead. Aliens (with little Newt being stranded for a month). Castaway.

Every one of these films involved a group or single guy getting himself stranded. I hesitate to even mention embassies because, quite frankly, the regulations in every one of them change like the wind every time a new administration comes along. And most people don't like the embarrassment that comes with asking Uncle Sam for help. People get bruised egos. Word gets out. They lose face. It can happen to anyone, me included, in endless ways.

A wallet goes missing. A passport. You can't access the bank account and God only knows why. When you try to backtrace your steps, your laptop gets stolen by a sweet Pinay named Ping Honeygirl. You chase that mud-flecked Pinay into a shanty and find a pack of dogs waiting for you led by Cujo the killer Pinoy.

In the event you do find yourself chasing some mud-flecked urchin... stop. Turn around. Go to the embassy of your respective country.

You'd be shocked at how easy it is to turn the tide away. I've friends from Britain, Canada and America and like me, they've all been in situations where, as my friend Pete from London says, "You can feel the Devil poke your rear," - and if you're seen chasing any waifs into the slums, you're doomed. It's a trap. It always is.

Go to the embassy instead. They'll help you get your laptop back and help you get home. In case you're wondering, the answer is no. They won't pay for it themselves unless they've exhausted every other option.

But that won't happen. Because what they'll do is sit you down and, after fixing you up with a nice cinnamon latte and glazed donut, will then proceed to give you the longest, most mentally exhaustive memory game you've ever had. They'll tell you to call every friend and relative you've ever known since third grade until you get enough funds for a plane ticket home. This works 99% of the time, and works well. There's no need to fleece the taxpayers since it's amazing what the human brain stores in the backroom that mysteriously comes to the surface when faced with a prospect of living in a shanty with Ping and Cujo.

The embassy has ways of digging up more than a few spare gold coins in your friend's coffers, at least until you reach that four-figure plane ticket price. So don't go sleeping with any Pinoy bums on the street before you've hit em up for some tax rebate love. That's why they're there: insurance for emergencies.

Remember: If you get stuck... beg, borrow or steal a ride to the embassy. Be warned, however, that this doesn't apply if you're arrested, which we'll discuss next.

Police

The first thing I noticed in Davao wasn't the lack of other 6'2 hack writers, or even people with European descent. It was the a lack of *tension* in my neck.

As I drove my Nuovo-Z motorbike close to the Marco Polo hotel, I noticed no speed traps to speak of.

Hmm, quite the oddity, I thought at the time.

Certainly it was different from Ontario, where speed traps were abundant but not that cleverly positioned. There, I loved to speed and speed fast when the snow melted. I never gave one lick what the speed limit was and I knew which roads to avoid and what to say to the cop to win him over. Well, most of the time.

Lots of sports car enthusiasts knew as well, and with all the long country roads to break in that new Camaro, resisting temptation was all but impossible. If you were a biker, forget it. The desire to inflame your ego and ride Ghost Rider each and every time was unstoppable.

But every once in a while in Ontario, I'd get a crick in my neck from scanning every corner as I looked for hidden cops. On the whole, policemen up here are more polite than in my native Louisiana. A little place called Abita Springs, just north of New Orleans, had the most corrupt cops you can imagine. Worse than Edwin Edwards. Worse than Huey Long. They'd give out tickets faster than a Willy Wonka did to the kids.

"Here's another sucker!"

I could almost sense the words as I slowed down - always too late. Once as a wayward teen, I'd contemplated gunning it. I'd barely seen the red blue, red blue of the lights before he shouted: "I've got a V8 in here! You can't outrun me!"

Davao, like much of the Philippines, wasn't like that at all. Speed traps weren't the main problem. Other things were. Like badly paved streets with potholes so deep they could swallow an elephant whole. The other was paying off corrupt cops. I kid you not. That's something you can get away with in the Philippines. You can't in Abita Springs, Louisiana. Believe me, I've tried.

In case you missed it, let me spell it out for you: You can BRIBE most officers you meet in the Philippines.

That is, without fear of being thrown in the slammer for five years. You cop a bribe in the USA and get caught, even a lowly $50 can be major trouble.

You get pulled over and say, "You know I'm DWI man,"...

...you've just started a forest fire. It's seen as sufficient evidence of intent, justifying conviction. In Texas, that kind of small-change bribery is a second-degree felony punishable by two to 20 years in prison and a $10,000 fine. Big money. When I tried it, I was lucky the cop was in a good mood since that was the day of his son's high school graduation. He still ticketed me, though.

It's a different story in the Philippines. A lot different. Whether you're in Davao or Cebu or Dumaguete, you want to slip that 200 peso bill right next to your license before he even exits his cruiser. No ifs, no buts. Be prepared and you won't need to say a word. But know that the longer you wait to perform this one simple little magic trick, the worse it's going to get for you. And believe me, cowboy, it always gets worse without the color green, since green'll mix quite nicely with blue and red but won't with black. You give em nothing but pitch black, you'll get nothing but trouble in return.

I'm dead serious. The longer you wait, the harder it'll be to get out of trouble, because more people will get involved (mostly bureaucrats), and cases can drag on for years and years over the simplest things you can imagine. Calling the embassy is a fool's errand. Once *they* get involved, you can forget about paying your way out. Those bureaucrats get their paws into it, and the only thing you'll be able to buy is a nice entertainment system in prison while they ensure you're being given due process. A lot of fat good that'll do you.

Embassies are good for many things, but playing judge and jury in third-world countries isn't one of them.

You're probably wondering which crimes you can bribe and which you can't. Well, for the most part it's the usual things you can spend a night in jail for. Punching someone in a bar. Getting a little too drunk and going slaphappy with a prostitute. Shoplifting. It's hit and miss but far more hit if you decide to ante up beforehand. You offer money to the first person you see with a badge, and you're on your way to less headaches.

Filipino cops love to chase bad guys like drug dealers and terrorists, but if you've damaged someone's property, give them an incentive to let it end right then and there. Doesn't matter if it's the other guy's fault or yours. Once lawyers get involved, it's like ringing Hell's dinner bell. Every scaly lawyer will want a piece of your hide. My advice is to give the first piece to the first officer and deny it to the rest. Most cops will want this as well.

Be firm, but deal with it politely and don't play the accuser's game of whose fault it is. That's like dancing with the devil and as we both know, the devil eventually comes for his due.

Street Kids

I've had my things stolen by thieves, pickpockets, Thai jet ski rentals and Craigslist ripoffs enough times to write a tome. It'd pass for good entertainment, I'd wager, if I could put my pride to rest. One thing my ego won't sit silent on, however, is the god awful amount of street kids that'll drain you dry. Allow me to relay the most important bit of advice you're ever going to hear about street kids in third world countries:

Nice guy never works. With any of them. It never has and never will.

What you see in Oliver! and Scrooge, where cute and skipping and singing runaways dance about like angels excited to get their new wings and halos, is pure nonsense. Runaways and orphans are cat-quick on their joints, yes, but they quickly learn the score as fast as any cat that's dumped on the streets.

I know because I took one in last winter up here. Some frumpy Fritz-looking cat dumped a litter right under my porch. Coyotes took two for dinner (just a hunch) but left the last one as some kind of sick joke. I thought of those hyenas from Lion King.

The next day the mother moved her. Over the course of three weeks, the mother disappeared and that lone kitten wandered on back to give me more affection than any girlfriend I'd ever dated in my life. I was hooked. That little claw edged it's way around my heart and refused to let go. So I took her in since, at the time, the only truly safe place was a spooky old tree next to my house. The same tree I'd caught her climbing down one morning.

So I named her Spooky.

Sinister-looking, yet as gentle as a lamb. Manila street kids? Not so much.

Cats learn quick. Even faster than humans do if put into a survival situation. Like which garbage cans to scour. Which restaurant back doors to milk for the leftovers. Which rodents go down easy. Which dogs are bark and no bite. And which country hicks'll take 'em in if they just poor on the lovin'.

Spooky knew the tricks of the trade. She was born with them.

Likewise, male street kids learn which tourists are the 'nice guy' variety or the 'church lady' who can't resist a cute face, and which ones aren't. It's an aura they can see and feel. A money vibe that few grownups can sense save for Benny Hinn types.

The girls are more like stray cats, ones that see ghosts. My own place rests on an old 1812 battleground and my cat sees the blasted ghostly buggers in wintertime.

Both girls and boys work in sync the way a couple of bank robbers would prior to a hit. First they case the joint. Study it. Analyze it. Ask the right questions, like how soft is the target? Response time? Competition? They memorize every camera, angle and distance to the cops until the day of execution - all so they can strike quick as lightning when the bank is weak and without hesitation. Hesitation is for the birds.

Which is why you should never hesitate around them. Ever. Strike before the iron gets hot so that the blade never gets close enough to slice into your ribs.

Dodging the Bullet

One fact of Filipino life I wish someone'd told me before I flew there is this:

Filipinos can own guns... but you as a foreigner cannot.

That means you can only rely on yourself to defend against a mob of gremlins. The nastier ones often have huge social networks they can call on to intimidate you with the press of a button, so tough guy tactics don't usually work without the cops getting involved. You don't need that headache. Most cops don't like pickpockets either, but between you and a pickpocket, they'll always choose cuteness over logic. See for yourself:

photo by Eric Gozar

For most of these cute little guys, especially the older lieutenants in the 12-14 age range, a man needs to be tough as nails because *they* are tough as nails. They've seen it all and sleep under the stars with rats and cats and bats. At least, the mouthy ones have.

Don't let their adorable catty eyes fool you. They can sense weakness and you'll need to counter this with a powerful **presence**. Be a walking, talking firebreather like General Patton, or the darkest, cruelest sorcerer that ever walked the earth so that not even one of these buggers gets to within four or five feet of you without feeling awe and fear. They need to smell it on your from afar the way a bear sniffs the air when it's a hundred feet out.

I'm pretty cold-hearted when it comes to thieves, but I've a friend in Cebu who is an absolute monster around them. Think Godzilla smoking a cigar, or R. Lee Armey's response to getting sassed by one of his Marine recruits. That's who you need to be. Proud and showing your warface when the situation dictates.

Most street kids are opportunistic boys who'll fleece you faster than Quicksilver can in the X-Men flicks. If he's engaging you in polite conversation and looks like he just stepped out of Oliver, watch out! You're the present target. The niceness is all an act. What that means is that 98% of them are the lowest of the low. They're micro-criminals that are as sharp as tacks and since the Philippines has very strict social laws against begging and thievery, well, you can imagine what they think of the penalty.

Showing them your strong side works better on boys than girls, curiously enough. The girls tend to work as couriers, or runners. Some are lookouts and some sit on the sidelines twirling their curls as the scroungy-faced males do all the hard work.

Over the years, many get used to the handouts and want more, so much that they begin to pickpocket those who refuse to give. Now they pickpocket everyone. It's far more lucrative that way, so you need to be so direct that they see the fires of Hell in your eyes and if they touch you, they're doomed.

The only caution here is situational awareness; observe, from the corner of your eye for instance, who is listening, who is watching, or recording. The last thing you want is a trio of jeepney nuns smacking your mouth with a flip-flop like that ruler nun did to the Blues Brothers. I watched in horror as that happened one hot night. It didn't end well for the guy.

Canada

There's a reason most people never follow up on their word to leave for Canada after the general election. Want to know why?

It's because of the perceived hassle.

A lot of the big name celebrities love to harp how they'll fly north to become snowbirds if their guy loses the election. They almost never do. The great irony here is that it's not much of a hassle at all. One simply has to *apply*, and most don't even do that because of this little habit called procrastination. Procrastination in 90% of the cases.

When I say 'apply,' that means applying for just about anything in Canada. A work visa. A student visa. A tourist visa. *Anything* to get those boosters warmed up to jet off to the great white north is views as too much hassle.

It's easy to read about others doing it and fantasize how much better Keanu Reeves and William Shatner's second life up here must be (not really), but most people are horrible at keeping their word. So they don't bother taking that all-important first step. They fidget. They sit and twiddle their thumbs like a couple of bored nuke guys who'd rather deal with a nuclear winter than a real winter. Better, they think, to deal with any fallout with SallieMae or the IRS - which in my view involves a little too much hair loss for my liking. God knows I've pulled out all of my own over their silly turnkey games.

That said, escaping to Canada isn't foolproof. It's just *impractical* for those chasing you. That's because for most collection agencies, it's just not financially worth it to chase you all the way to Newfoundland or Nunavut. It's much easier to bluff their way into your bank account in the grand ol' USA by hurling fiery threats like darts until you finally cave. Most do. The final threat usually goes something like this:

"Unless you grant us unfettered access to your account, by 5PM today, we'll send in a SEAL team headed up by Bruce Willis to take you out."

Well, maybe not *you* per se, but certainly your house. One aspect to student loans I've noticed over the last few years creeping into U.S. student loans (bank contracts), are liens. Liens on your house. Liens written with such nefariousness as to have been written by the Devil himself.

One instance involved a grandmother who'd co-signed for her granddaughter's student loan. Only when grandma died, the loan became fully due. All of it. Worse than this was that they'd placed a $20,000 lien on her grandmother's house. The granddaughter's mother only found this out when she researched the county records on her mother's estate. Imagine her shock. If the daughter had been the one to pass on to that great gig in the sky, well then it'd be 77 year old Betsy that would've had to cough it all up. Pronto.

Now that's the kind of debt that'd shoot me northward no matter what crazy winter those Canucks were having. But moving to Canada to escape debt won't do you any good if you work for an American company. If they find you, they'll make your workplace as miserable as the Ninth Circle of Hell. Hellhounds, those people.

On the other hand, if we're talking about something other than debt, like for instance - running from a crime like "kidnapping," well that's something else and much harder to get away with.

If you want to run to Canada to escape a crime committed in the USA, and you know nothing about how to disappear, how to stay disappeared, or have little in the way of connections like relatives and friends, then you'd better be Jeremiah "liver eating" Johnson and know how to trap beaver, scale a mountain and survive in sub-zero freezing temperatures and live off the grid. More on that in a moment, but first let's discuss asylum in general and what the Canadian Mounties might do if pressed by Uncle Sam to serve you up with a side of Canadian bacon.

Escape from New York

There's a funny scene in the film *Escape From New York,* where Van Cleef's character, a real hang 'em high supercop kind of guy named Hauk, threatens Snake Plisskan if he so much as thinks of turning his loaned police glider around and flying off to Canada. The guy is more chock full o' nuts than even Snake. By a country mile.

"If you get back in that glider, I'll burn you off the wall!" Hauk yells into the com at police HQ, just as Snake contemplates aborting the mission. It's implied that someone's had the President for dinner at the crash site.

It's also implied that Snake could, if he wanted to, apply for asylum once he flies off to Canada. Back when I saw the flick in theaters in 1980, I was a bit skeptical. Yet here we are in 2015, and Canada is a very different story. First of all, Canada's since given up granting asylum to Americans. I nevertheless got a good laugh at the thought of them granting it to a bank robbing, gun-dealing, ex-Special Forces hustler like Snake Plisskan - a guy who'd have you strangled in your sleep if you double-crossed him.

And Snake just may have been that desperate. Who knows. Desperate people do some pretty stupid things but what gets them in a knot is neglecting to plan out their escape to the last detail. They short themselves. That's kind of what happened to poor Snake. A half-baked plan to save the President from a drug kingpin called The Duke, who rules over the prison system of New York with an iron fist and all with only one man and one gun. No police backup. No eye in the sky. Yep, that'll work.

Not that it'd matter in Snake's case even if he could evade Hauk's drones - which Hauk didn't have. Canada'd ship Snake back no matter what crime he'd committed. If he hummed a copyrighted song and the States didn't like it, they'd send him back pronto.

Oh they'd be nice about it, I'll grant 'em that. Like maybe handcuff him in a coffin, but pack it so tight with bottles of Canadian maple syrup that he'd dream of Dudley Do Right for the next half century. After that, they'd throw in some Tim Horton's donuts and escort him the same way Boba Fett did with Han Solo. Ice cold and locked tighter than Fort Knox. Hauk would've loved that. Glazed Timbits with a side of snake.

Canada is a no-fly zone if ever you're in serious, deep trouble unless you've got top notch connections, and by that I mean off-the-grid connections.

They turned over Mark Emery, eminent marijuana activist and he was one of their own. Other Canadian judges have been known to extradite their fellow Canadians for more serious crimes, one of whom was a young Canadian who'd never set foot in the States. The deed in question? He emailed child porn, 38 pics in all, to an undercover Homeland Security agent after the agent hounded him to do it for weeks. The guy was sentenced to 8 and a half years to serve in the land of the free. All on account of the extradition treaty.

On that point, just because a country does *not* have an extradition treaty with the USA <u>does not mean</u> they won't extradite you if you're wanted on a felony charge. Like kidnapping your own kid from an abusive spouse, for example. You show up at any airport in Canada or cross the border, your face'll pop up faster than generic Canadian pop tarts.

<u>Sanctuary Countries</u>

Before I go into tactics that could theoretically help you disappear in Canada, I've compiled a list of alternative countries where you'd stand a much higher chance of hiding. Remember, good connections are lifesavers. In the case of Syria, disappearance can be a world of hurt if you don't have good underground connections. The others depend on whom you know and more importantly, who you know that trusts you enough to put their own freedom on the line. You've got to really have their trust before you run.

Here's the list:

Afghanistan, Algeria, Andorra, Angola, Armenia, Bahrain, Bangladesh, Belarus, Bosnia, Herzegovina, Brunei, Burkina Faso, Burma, Burundi, Cambodia, Cameroon, Cape Verde, the Central African Republic, Chad, China, Comoros, Congo, Djibouti, Equatorial Guinea, Eritrea, Ethiopia, Gabon, Guinea, Guinea-Bissau, Indonesia, Ivory Coast, Kazakhstan, Kosovo, Kuwait, Laos, Lebanon, Libya, Macedonia, Madagascar, Maldives, Mali, Marshall Islands, Mauritania, Micronesia, Moldova, Mongolia,

Montenegro, Morocco, Mozambique, Namibia, Nepal, Niger, Oman, Qatar, Russia, Rwanda, Samoa, São Tomé & Príncipe, Saudi Arabia, Senegal, Serbia, Somalia, Sudan, Syria, Togo, Tunisia, Uganda, Ukraine, United Arab Emirates, Uzbekistan, Vanuatu, Vatican, and Vietnam.

- In the case of Cambodia, we saw they quite willingly handed over Pirate Bay founder Gottfrid Svartholm to Sweden, though why he would want to live in Cambodia when Sweden prisons are as posh as they are is another discussion.

- We saw Edward Snowden run to Russia when the heat was on, catching a flight from Hong Kong and later requesting (and being granted) temporary asylum.

- Fredrik 'Pirate Bay' Neij's country of choice was Laos, after being sentenced to a whopping one year in a Swedish prison and ordered to pay $905,000 in "damages." Laos refused to hand him over. Later, in November 2014, Neij was arrested on an Interpol warrant as he attempted to cross into Thailand. Eventually, even smart guys get bored of hiding in a jungle, I suppose.

Costa Rica may be another option for you.

There've been a few high-profile cases of runners making it there, but you need to do your research beforehand like anywhere else. Know the differences in culture between their country and your own. Know the history of extraditions to your native country. Know how to get out fast if a revolution erupts, or a volcano.

Everything safe costs money, so you need to have a substantial savings and a portfolio that is diversified enough so that you have some way to make bank, without using a bank. Some way to lock it up from prying eyes so they can't raid your account over something like student loans. If that happens, as it does all too frequently in the USA, you'll get no advance warning unless you've got an inside friend who works at the bank and watches your account 24/7. Most people on the run don't have that luxury.

But I'll admit that you're more likely to make allies in Canada than in the above countries since the culture is almost a carbon copy of the U.S.

Border Officers and Encrypted Laptops

I remember some of my fellow math students offering to commit seppuku rather than battle the dreaded math final. It was a kamikaze mission for many students, myself included. I offered to fall on my sword to my old math teacher, Ms. Needles, as well. She declined. Take it, she said, or take a semester off and a date with the coach's paddle (rumored to have bent nails in it). That old bat could scare an orc chieftain straight. Not kidding.

Sixth period came to be known as the satanic hour by my junior high crew. Being after lunch, our heads were still swirling with D&D imagery; it was the hour of divas with downturned horns and succubi and every unclean spirit you could imagine from every D&D board game you can imagine. All the good ones, anyway. It's funny thinking back on it, how every class *prior* to that hour of cacophony was a class of maddening ticking. The clocks I mean. They were that annoying. Like a pigeon pecking your ankle as you dangled off a cliff.

Tick... tick... tick...

A ticking time bomb was easier to listen to. I soon began to appreciate what submarine sonar guys dealt as they navigated all those mines in WWII.

Math was never my strong point to begin with. It only seemed to strengthen my repertoire of new F bombs over any real math improvement, so I never saw the point. Every equation looked like Ds and Fs. Working them out was like juggling grenades in a clown's dressing room. Booom. Little fires everywhere.

Procrastination became a real problem.

I only wished I'd dealt with it much sooner than I did. Reason being, is that I viewed encryption the same way. Only I'd learned later on that if I intended on traveling internationally to some of my dream destinations halfway across the globe, then it was required. Big time. I'd have to learn it if I was going to keep other people's noses out of my private life.

Since then, I've found that good luck and fortune often arrive unannounced, and for this reason you need to assume that there's a possibility that you'll become a jet-setting digital nomad warrior someday - with sensitive files on your device. Maybe you're not Donald Trump, but someone computer-savvy who loves to travel and absorb new cultures and live off his laptop. That's fine. Just don't make the mistake I did. All those years ago, I shunned encryption because I erroneously decided that learning how to encrypt my laptop was akin to working out those math gremlins I so hated in my youth.

Before we dive into encryption, let's discuss Canadian Border Services. Or rather, what they can and can't do to you. If you're going to make a mistake, better it's here than overseas. And if you cite constitutional rights and insist they've no legal standing to confiscate your laptop, go ahead and toss it over Niagara Falls. You'll retrieve it quicker than you will the RCMP.

First, bringing any kind of gun or even a knife across the Canadian border can be a serious offense - at both ends. Notice I said 'can be', not 'is always'. It really depends on who you are and what your situation is and above all, if you're polite.

Marines have been arrested in Mexico with nothing but a shotgun in the back of their pickup truck. In Canada though, American police have even been arrested for forgetting to check their handguns into secondary inspection. Ever since Marc Lépine shot up a school in Montreal way back in 1989 over what he perceived as feminists stealing his career as an engineer, Canada's made it 1000 times more difficult to own a firearm. I'd even say it's 10,000 times more difficult to bring one in from the States without informing them first.

Not that you'd *want* to smuggle one in of course, since most crimes in Canada involve grand theft and shoplifting. Canadians are also world renown for being friendly to outsiders, so you needn't worry like you'd worry in Detroit.

It's what lies in places like Banff Park, or way out in the Yukon that demand gun ownership. You'll wish you had one if you run into a grizzly, believe me. By the time that Yogi Bear is on you, you won't have time to fish any handgun out of your backpack. You *might* have time to get to your shotgun.

It isn't just grizzlies that require guns. A few smugglers operate here and there, mostly flying in tobacco and other frowned-upon goods. But those guys'll leave you alone if you leave them alone since this isn't exactly Juarez, Mexico. For grizzlies, forget it. Follow the three 'S's: Shoot, Shovel and Shut up.

Smuggling items into Canada requires a cunning mind, the kind that'd put Jabba the Hutt out of business. It's not to be taken lightly. Stories abound of guys who thought they were smarter and quicker on the draw than law enforcement. If a Border Officer had any business sense, he could self-publish a collection and hit the bestseller chart in less than a week. None have. But there's that many dummies out there who want to be Han Solo sporting a Canadian tuque.

One story involved a Canadian teenager who, while at the border, sobbed like a little baby when the officer asked him if he'd smuggled in any weapons. Much like the 'Father, I confess!' scene from The Godfather, the kid admitted how he'd gotten into some trouble down south at a bachelor party, and found himself stuck with a handgun he'd never laid eyes upon. When sent to secondary checkpoint, it turned out his gun was a BB gun. His 'friends' had played a delicious joke on him, telling him he'd killed a hooker. Ha, good ol' Southern Comfort.

Now then. You're probably wondering what tips a border guard them off. Well, contrary to popular belief, Border Officers on the Canadian side don't know your entire life history when they scan your passport. When you drive through a Canadian checkpoint, here's what happens:

Your passport is scanned (the part that has all the '<' left arrow symbols) using an international-standard that's easily readable by a CBSA language named IPIL. This searches through law enforcement records such as outstanding warrants, both present and past, and beyond this, there's just no time to go through every database with the lineup these guys have to deal with. It just takes way too much time. Planes land every day with a 1000 Canadians who are eager to get home and into a hot tub.

The shortcut to seeing if you're a criminal or not isn't by searching databases, as useful as they are. The way to tell deception is by studying your *behavior*:

Tics. Facial changes. Visual cues. Jittery drumming fingers. There's other dead giveaways, too. Like:

Where are your eyes? That's the first clue.

During a drug raid, DEA agents will often check where you look to see if you'll give up the drug location. Other things come into play as well:

- Tone.
- Hesitation.
- Nervous feet.

You'd be surprised what a seasoned smuggler will give away when pressed by a Sam Elliot lookalike and a gruff voice. They get nervous. They loosen up and squirm and start talking just to fill the air with something that takes the stress off.

They can't help it really. It's just hard-wired into some people's brains to get nervous whenever authority is around. Oh I'll wager a few may get better at hiding the signs if they've smuggled for eons, assuming they're not rotting in jail.

Whatever you need to smuggle across the border; exotic lizards or Blue Bell Homemade Vanilla Ice Cream or clown shoes - if you act nervous, the jig is up and you're going to secondary inspection unless you decide to run the gate, in which case they'll shoot you.

They know the difference between fatigue and nervousness. They've seen it all and heard it all. The chances that you'll get a wet-behind-the-ears rookie is slim to none, so don't count on that.

However, that doesn't mean you need to be a jerk to a guy in a badge simply because he's wearing a badge. I've been tempted to repay attitude with attitude plenty of times myself, but doing so only causes problems and some of those guys deliberately do this by design to get you to lose focus and trip you up in your speech.

That's not to say that being an absolute jerk to the officer will put you on any blacklist. It won't. If you've got dual citizenship, all the better since they have to let you in as a Canadian since that's what the Canadian Charter dictates. What they don't have to let in is *your stuff.*

So what *will* put you on their blacklist? Any of the following:

- Shipping drugs by mail
- Refusing to report to secondary inspection.
- Lying (aka 'Making a False Declaration' - if you lie to one officer at the Vancouver station, the one at Niagara Falls will know about it).
- Having *any* bad history at the border.

And the best one saved for last:

- Not giving up the password to your encrypted laptop.

They'll let *you* through, sure, but not your beloved laptop. They don't even need a warrant at all to search your phone, your Samsung Galaxy Tab or Ipad or any electronic device.

You may be thinking at this point that encryption can really be a bane or a boon, and you'd be right. But it's always better to encrypt than to not encrypt. Better still, install a fake (encrypted) operating system that sits atop your real one.

Why?

Because you absolutely, unequivocably want to give them *something* that makes you *look like you have nothing to hide*. The other reason is to satisfy their ego. They want to feel like they're doing their job and if they can get you to cough up your password, then it's mission accomplished.

Now, you don't have to look like a schmuck. You simply have to look like a professional who values your privacy. They won't sit down and fine-comb your files since they've got programs available to search for signatures on digital files (aka hash files).

Another thing to remember is this: You need to lock down your data *before*, not after, your arrival at the border station. Designate a section of your hard drive so that it's encrypted out of an officer's plain sight, and with a second encryption key. There you'll store your private files. Files like:

- Photos of the Filipina lovelies
- Transcripts, scanned tax forms, UFO photos
- Recordings of you and Edward Snowden

Furthermore, you should do this even if you have full disk encryption. Diskcryptor (diskcryptor.net) offer hidden partitions as well as most older encryption applications like PGP and Drivecrypt and Veracrypt.

Even if you follow the above to the letter, know that Border officers aren't forensics experts. Most of them don't have the mental fortitude to go through your entire Windows or Linux system to see if you've got one encrypted file that's fifty gigs in size or five megabytes. If they want to "image" your hard drive, that's no sweat off your back as long as your real password is good and the decoy one looks real enough to fool anyone short of a forensics expert.

Time is priceless where encryption is concerned, but it takes way too long to do it at the 11th hour.

If you're on your way to the border station from the airport, say from Buffalo, NY to the Canadian Border Station at Niagara Falls, it may be too late to encrypt anything. Do it **before** you get on the plane. You need to have that decoy ready to show, with *recent* activity, in case they want to boot up the operating system. It may just look suspicious if the decoy Windows or Linux hasn't been used in a month. Perhaps not to *every* customs agent, but there may be one smart cookie in the batch who knows all about decoy operating systems on hidden partitions.

Though you'll probably get Deputy Fife over some CSI expert who knows a dozen programming languages and has hacked the Pentagon looking for UFOs.

Lastly, store nothing incriminating on that decoy operating system. What's illegal in Canada might not be in the USA. For Canada, especially, don't be cute and paste-in freaky underage cat-girl anime of any kind, no matter how much your Japanese girlfriend likes it. Vanilla bookmarks only.

No social media. Then put in a nice backdrop, not the stock wallpaper that comes with a Windows or Linux install.

There's a few other sobering topics of note, the first of which comes from the ANSSI (French Government IT-Security) who has some good advice for travelers (most of which must be observed **before** you ever set foot on a plane):

- Wherever you're going, know the country's confiscation laws.
- Use devices made for travel, but don't load any extra-mission data.
- Backup all relevant data *before* the flight in a safe place (bears repeating)
- Never bring sensitive data if you can help it.
- Use a VPN to upload and retrieve data *instead of* bringing it across the border
- If flying, use a screen filter to stop Neb the tax accountant neighbor from spying.
- Never plug your laptop back into the company's network after having been seized without giving it a thorough examination.

As stated before: If any border guard takes your laptop and demands the encryption password, politely give him the decoy pass. Never refuse unless you can afford to lose your laptop. Further, if you've got no decoy operating system and you must give him the real deal, inform your business partners as soon as possible so as to revoke any passwords/certs/non-local IP access before going into damage control.

Now let's discuss tampering by officials.

One way to verify if your laptop's been tampered with, is to cover the screws under the laptop with *glitter polish*. Then take a high-resolution picture after it sets. It's impossible for an airport security guard to repaint that exact pattern of stars after having unplugged the internal drive for copying. If someone's cloned your hard drive, compare the picture with what you see. You'll know if it's contaminated. In fact I'd say if you lost control of your laptop somewhere along the way, you should treat it as if it passed through North Korea and is loaded up with every strain of spyware you can imagine.

The best advice that I've ever heard came from a Filipino restaurant owner in Dumaguete, and it's this:

Change every password upon your return. Scammers abound in places like Manila and Bangkok, and just because you used your debit card in a fancy-pants Thai eatery with Bruce Campbell as sharks and sucker fish swam underneath your feet doesn't mean you weren't taken for a ride.

Cons of Canada

Encrypted laptops and grumpy border officers are easy peasy next to some of the other negatives of that wintery country. It can put a Louisiana guy in a hot tailspin. It certainly did mine when I moved to Ontario in 2002. It was a whole other way of life than what I was accustomed to, not the least of which is their lack of good Mexican restaurants.

And that's not to say that it's any one thing, either, but rather a lot of little things; warm and cold fronts if you will, that, when stacked atop one another add up to one nasty hurricane of headaches. This is especially true if you're from somewhere like the Florida Keys. This is true no matter which country you flee to, but most people think Canada is a clone of the USA - which it clearly isn't.

First off, it's more expensive to live in Canada than in almost any place in the States except Manhattan. Montreal is nice, but very expensive. Cell phone plans in that beautiful city are through the roof since the government regulates it.

There other things. A case of beer can cost $35 dollars. Handguns are illegal. Unemployment is high in many places, especially Ontario. Newfoundland is perhaps the worst place to be jobless so if you're going to work there then it's best to do so from your laptop. The same way you'd do it in the Philippines.

The main negative though, is the brutal cold you must endure no matter the province. Think arctic glacier ice fishing cold. And you'll know it come November just as surely as if someone shot you with a shrink-ray gun and plopped your naked body into an ice cold mug of Rickard's Red beer.

Travel is slow. If you're ever unfortunate enough to drive over black ice in wintertime, it'll be too late once it dawns on you what it is. This has happened to me countless times and I think it's shaved off 5 years of my life with every incident. You touch the brakes, you're sideways and in the ditch. Heaven help you if this happens while you're on the Lewiston-Queenston Bridge, proud sponsor of a 400 foot drop straight down. Every time I cross that beast I'm reminded of why Dukes of Hazzard episodes are scarce up here. It ain't because of the flag.

Can you picture the General Lee doing 80 in a 20 with a broken ice bridge up ahead and sporting a red maple leaf instead of a confederate flag and popping up surrounded by Canadian beaver? Neither can I.

Here's the raw data, in USD:

Rent Per Month
Apartment (1 bedroom) in City Centre $736.39
Apartment (1 bedroom) Outside of Centre $505.18
Apartment (3 bedrooms) in City Centre $1,364.56
Apartment (3 bedrooms) Outside of Centre $848.72

Utilities
Basic (Electric, Heat, Water, Garbage) for 900 sq. ft Apt
   $86.79
1 min. of Prepaid Mobile Tariff Local (No Discounts or Plans) $0.27
Internet (10 Mbps, Unlimited) $37.97

Restaurants
Meal, Inexpensive Restaurant $9.26
Meal for 2, Mid-range Restaurant, Three-course $38.58

McMeal at McDonalds $6.95
Domestic Beer $3.86

Sports And Leisure
Fitness Club, Monthly Fee for 1 Adult $37.37
Tennis Court Rent (1 Hour) $9.65
Cinema, 1 Ticket $9.26

Salary

Average Monthly Disposable Salary (After Tax)
$2,129.14

Montreal

As you can see, the average salary seems quite low for the higher rent you must pay, but the pluses of blending in, and in a magnificent city like Montreal (if you can wing it), far outweigh the negatives.

Cost of Living - Its much more expensive to live in Toronto or Vancouver than in Montreal. Rent is cheap and you don't need a car. The public transit system makes for good anonymity if you pay cash, and you'll save thousands using it. It's also biker-friendly and if you're trying to disappear, learn cycling!

Culture - My first night walking around in downtown Montreal was one of amazement. The cobblestone pathways and boutiques everywhere reminded me of the French Quarter in New Orleans, only a lot cleaner and the women far more beautiful than any I'd seen in the South. It seemed very European and moreover, the people here work to live, not live to work.

Anonymity Friendly - Montreal attracts artists like flowers attract bees. It's been over twenty years since my thespian days in high school, but if I were so inclined to rekindle that flame, Montreal'd be my number one destination on the list. There's tons of opportunity to pursue acting gigs, modeling or music avenues. Being an anonymous artist is a lot easier than being an anonymous code monkey working in San Francisco.

Festivals - With almost 100 festivals per year (see tourisme-montreal.org), it's easy to be a cash only guy year round and forgo the internet completely. No internet means no tracking. It makes for a nice place to restart your life without data mining or skip tracers hunting you down.

French - Learning a new language can go a long way towards giving you a new identity, but Montreal French is not the same as Paris French. There are quirks in the language that, if you ignore them, can reveal your origin and uncover an old identity you're trying to bury.

Words like liquide, foufounnes and gosses, for example, have different meanings than what you may think. Some ask questions by *intonation* over subject/verb method (as tu vs. tu as) in a very Italian-like way. You'll also learn quickly that Quebecois-French carries more of a monotone vibe than Paris-French, but Paris-French uses more English words. Then there are idioms like 'Vente de garage' vs. 'Vente au garage' (since you're not actually selling a garage, right?).

And there's accents. These are hard to learn and if you try and fake it, your cover can be blown. Many variations exist throughout Canada, with Acadians sounding very different (and confusing) than what I heard in the bayou of Houma, Louisiana - where Acadian means something else. You'll eventually pick it up if you practice, but it's a catch-22 since practicing on strangers slowly dissolves any anonymity you've built up. People will take notice unless you've a good cover story and backcover to support it.

Money

The French language isn't the only issue if you decide to run to Montreal. There are other issues. Like money. Successfully disappearing requires lots of it, and the more money you have, the higher your chances of success. Unless you plan on going into the escort business, my advice is to save as much as you can *before* you run so that there's no surprises waiting for you behind the maple leafed door.

Technology also costs money. It's too bad that we can't just pay a fee and have our online identity erased. That grumpy old man called The Internet won't allow it, I suspect, because it's built to preserve rather than to erase. To that, it's allergic to just about any kind of deletion or forgiveness or even a fiftieth-year Jubilee as practiced in the Old Testament. It's one giant memory chip storing everything you think, love, hate or lust over and we can't force it to forget about us. It sucks.

The silver lining is barely visible, but it's there, and it's this: What we have to overcome is *heuristic-analysis*. Every tracker, every cookie, every app is built with some kind of heuristics in mind. Picture this: You're walking along in downtown Montreal and texting your new girlfriend and oblivious to the fact that even your Firefox browser can be fingerprinted from afar by all the addons you use, the resolutions, the bookmarks, the font settings, and the frequency with which you alter them. Not exactly romantic.

Next you need to deal with your offline personas, since most shops you hang out at employ their own tracking mechanisms. They know what you buy. How much of it. Which brands. You didn't think they gave you that loyalty card because you're handsome, did you? They use it for tracking you and building a profile so as to better target you with ads.

Killing off heuristic-tracking means you have to switch up everything you do almost 100%. Cease using the same apps, the same accounts, even buying the same food from the same brands. For groceries, this can be simple if you're moving from Scottsdale, Arizona to Montreal, Quebec, since they often don't sell the same brands. In fact, I'm still seething that I can't get Blue Bell Homemade Ice Cream in Canada unless I go to Outback Steakhouse.

Poisoning the Old Self

No one said spycraft was easy.

If you think learning how to be anonymous online is hard, try doing it offline. Going dark and *staying* dark is tougher than nails to do off the grid and in a way that isn't obvious. It takes a problem-solver to do it right. An analyst. A critical thinker who can see problems coming way off in the distance like John the Baptist could out in that fire roasted desert. Yet you and I know that even he made mistakes, the last of which cost him his head. He probably saw it coming, too, but perhaps decided he'd had enough heat for one lifetime.

None of us are desert prophets, though, and I dare say that offline people are very far from being anything like the brass-balls John the Baptist. Most can be the most gutless weenies in the world if they so much as see a pizza made of crickets, never mind eating it. My sister eats them and it drives me nuts. She wield's that power over me like a lightning bolt, always rubbing it in. When I saw one of those in New York and began a taste-test, I nearly ralphed my breakfast. Only I never made a big stink about it because to be honest, it was kind of embarrassing since everyone else had eaten one. I'd become quite the weenie myself, so I mosied on over to a hot dog stand and was in pure Heaven.

Now, if it'd been an online discussion? Well I would've acted like Thor himself! Bolts n hammers and all. Heck, some people can be tougher than *Oden* in some of the forums I've visited.

Yep, that Oden. Angry Oden that rages against his keyboard, where every keystroke is a lightning-filled ban-hammer full of sound and fury but pretty much made of nothing where humans are concerned. That's because the false sense of anonymity the internet gives you comes with a terrible side effect: Overconfidence.

Overconfidence and general cockiness mixes about as well with privacy as oil does with water. You get careless online and say something to the wrong person or group, you may get pinched if the site owner is a backstabbing weenie who's tough online but a weenie in person.

We all know that Tor hides our IP addresses and that it's a great tool to use to disappear online. But it can't erase old photos of us. To that, any photos you've ever uploaded to a social media site like Facebook or Twitter will in all likelihood stay there, forever.

Christ may even return before they get around to deleting them. Even messages you've written in a Usenet newsgroup in 1998, or the Ars Technica forum, even if it was years ago, will still be there decades out. Mark my words.

Yet even *one picture* linked to your new identity by some busybody on the street can undermine everything. A random snapshot, say, uploaded to Facebook with you making that funny parrot face in the background. It's quite the photo bomb if you're trying to stay invisible.

Getting rid of it seems like an impossible mission to most, and I'd agree. It mostly is. We can't exactly go to every site and delete the info ourselves without the magic keys, and most administrators of those sites have sky-high egos as it is. You'd sooner be granted permission by the Almighty to steal your kid sister's hamster named Boo and chuck it to the Devil's inner circle before they'd delete some embarrassing tidbit you spat out years ago.

But something we *can* do is change *elements* of our old identity, so that any data sets tracking the old 'you' become stale and unusable. Sort of like having a covert group in which every member knows a secret value that non-members don't. For example, Expelling one member requires changing the secret value. If the expelled member doesn't know the new value, it's game over. He's out because he's got poisoned, outdated data.

Earlier in the book, we saw how to delete data permanently on most social media sites. What we didn't cover is that many websites like Google and Facebook don't really delete anything. They retain your data to sell to the highest bidder. Canada for instance, has strong privacy laws and 'Do Not Call' lists. That doesn't stop telemarketers from calling you at dinnertime, does it? No way. They call anyway, any old time they feel like it. It's a sad fact that many may get more calls from simply being on a Do Not Call list. A way we can undermine this is by injecting fake data into the tracking stream. Here's how.

I.) Create a list of every social media site or forum account that's linked to you.

II.) Tweak any personal info about you, your friendships, your family, by adding **false data**. Then Unlink your related accounts, but *relink* them to ones that point to something (or someone) else. Change every detail. 'Unlike' things you wouldn't normally like. Swap email addresses with fictional ones. Be certain that no link exists between any of the 'poisoned' accounts.

III.) Then allow the poison to do its work. Slowly but surely, the data stream will become saturated with false leads that end to nowhere. This is helpful if you want to skip out on skip tracers or collection agencies.

If you wait a month or two for the search engines to kick in, you can then delete the accounts altogether. They won't really be deleted of course, but the data contained within will be chock full of nutty information that's not worth a hill of beans to anyone.

Another option is to use the anonymous network tool called Tor, or a VPN connection to search for your name. I tried this myself and found three people in North America with my exact name. One was a lawyer in Tennessee that even shared my middle name. Only he looked a lot like Eddie Munster, and even sported an Eddie Munster haircut. Kinda like Neil Cavuto from FoxNews. I kid you not.

Anyway, if you wanted to you could link all your information to point to this other person. Sort of like an inverted identity switch.

Now then. It goes without saying that if you want to stay invisible that you need to avoid Facebook. One reason is that Facebook, as well as many other social media sites, have every users' contact lists due to the way mobile apps read data. Once the data gets sent back to HQ and cross-referenced, all that must be done is to sort through those contact lists to find people that have your number. Cover blown.

Thailand

It came as quite the shock to see how spectacular the skyline was at Sirocco's restaurant in Bangkok. I stared awestruck for ten minutes. The waiter tapped my shoulder several times, but I shooed his hand away, hoping to see if one of those flying 'Spinner' cars from Blade Runner would zip by.

By the time I opened my mouth to speak, I'd forgotten how flimsy my Thai ability was. Luckily for me, his English far surpassed my Thai (if your Thai is lacking, he'll switch you over to English faster than you can say Dr. Eldon Tyrell).

After I'd exhaled, he grinned as he said, "That look on your face. We see a lot. Blush response." He blinked several times. "Fluctuation of pupil. Dilated iris. You like our city?"

I nodded as I did indeed, though he'd clearly gotten used to the futurist visuals and noir rainscape. "Good!" he replied. "You come back with wife next time so not take our pretty pretty women."

Stories below, it was a different story completely with all the crazy wires everywhere. I made darn sure not to step anywhere near wires or open puddles in the rain.

A common mention in expat forums is that you don't need to know any Thai to get around. I can tell that claim is false. You can't even 'get by' without speaking Thai. No matter where you are - Bangkok, Chiang Mai, Phukut - you need the language to get around because frankly, it's hard enough being a stranger in a strange land without expecting everyone to decipher your drunken sign language. For a disappearing act, all the moreso. This was the most glaring difference between Thailand and the Philippines.

The rent and expense is a notch higher, but still far lower than in the West, with the best part being the biggest bang for your buck in Bangkok you can imagine.

Thailand Expenses

Rent in Bangkok is more expensive than in the Philippines, but not much more. For the first-world technology you get, it makes it far worth it to splurge a little more for the added reliability, as long as you don't mind the rain every other day. And some places like Chiang Mai may just shock you with their insanely low prices. You'll wonder how they manage to stay in business. But they do, even though on occasion the power'll go out and as you look out the window, you'll see a jungle of internet wires that no one could ever hope to untangle.

But they do. And quickly. And almost always before you can log a complaint.

In Dumaguete, I met a few Pinoy landlords who'd lament how western guys always 'complained' about the living conditions. In Bangkok, I never heard this at all. If you're complaining about a leaky faucet or mold or whatever to your tenant, you'll get prompt action. No waiting games.

Rent Per Month
Apartment (1 bedroom) in City Center $589.57
Apartment (1 bedroom) Outside of Center $318.34
Apartment (3 bedrooms) in City Center $1,746.38

Restaurants

Meal, Inexpensive Restaurant $1.48

Meal for 2, Mid-range Restaurant, Three-course $17.81

McMeal at McDonalds $4.45

Utilities
Basic (Electric, Heat, Water, Garbage) for Apartment
$107.10
1 min. of Prepaid Mobile   0.04
Internet (6 Mbps, Unlimited Data, Cable/ADSL) $18.82

Clothing
1 Pair of Jeans (Levis 501) $84.48
1 Summer Dress in a Chain Store (Zara, H&M, ...) $53.56

1 Pair of Nike Running Shoes (Mid-Range) $102.00

Two things jump out at me. One is the price for a nice restaurant, which obviously target out-of-towners with money to blow. Nothing too surprising there. The other is clothing. In the Philippines I saw a lot of counterfeit goods, and not just with electronic products but with many other things. While the clothing in Thailand was decent compared to Manila, what I bought at the SM Mall in Davao was downright robbery. Every shirt I bought had a tendency to rip, tear or otherwise deteriorate the moment the weekend hit, as though the threads themselves were made of splinter-thick fish bones.

Safety Issues

While I was never mugged in the Philippines, there were times when I wished I'd flown to Bangkok instead just to avoid the safety issues. During my Cebu trip, I noticed armed guards outside almost every store I entered, over 80% of which carried machine guns.

In Bangkok, a person can wear whatever they want without fear of getting hoodwinked by hordes of pickpocketing jawas. In fact I'd even recommend a guy suit up for most high end restaurants and bars in any major Thai city, without fear of anything save for getting hit by some Thai running with a box of chickens over his head. Wear a Gucci watch if you wish. A nice suit. Go out slim n' trim.

The following are a few pointers that just may save your life.

• Cut your normal drink usage by half if it's a new establishment. Drink bills add up at an exponential rate in Bangkok. A ten dollar bill may just turn into a hundred dollar bill by the end of the night. In the shadier places, they'll do a lot more to you than make you wash the dishes should you come up empty-handed come dawn.

• Buy a lock for your bike. Any bike. I've heard of cases where a bike rental place will hire some thai street kid to steal the bike and then charge *you* for the crime they committed!

• If they ask for a passport before you can rent a motorbike, give them a copy only. If they insist on the real deal... walk out. They're trying to fleece you. Besides, you'll need your real one if you're pulled over by a cop.

• Thai cabs and tuk tuk guys are a lot like Filipino cab drivers. You get in and the scam starts with, 'For you my American friend, I give you my special discounted price!'. Only it's higher than what any other Thai would pay. Be cautious but discuss it prior to taking off.

• If a Thai starts a fight with you in the middle of the street and generally acts like a crazy person... he is. Most Thai men are laid back and shy. Run, don't walk, if you encounter someone you think may have just snorted battery acid. You're a walking ATM to him and about to have a close encounter with a baseball bat from his partner hiding in an alley.

Opsec in Thailand

The more you sweat in peace, the less you bleed in war.
Those were Norman Schwarzkopf's words. And there as
true to life as the sky is blue.

If you're in Thailand and you find yourself 'settling in' as it
were, be carful not to allow the pretty blue liquor in the
flaming shot glass to turn your lips into a blabber-mouth
purple dinosaur. Loose lips, I mean. We covered this in a
previous chapter, but I forgot one important history link,
and that is to never 'sweat in peace' by taking the same
risks the PIRA (Provisional Irish Republican Army) took
in 1971. It was an OPSEC disaster; one that exposed more
than a few underground members to British intelligence.
Here are the mistakes they made in case you're not up on
Irish history:

- Shouting IRA songs in bars - so loud that people outside
could hear them.

- Bar bragging about successful operations vs. failures -
and *publicly* pointing blame while drunk. Recall the Secret
Service agents in South America when one agent got cheap
with one of the escorts while drunk.

- Not wearing disguises during IRA protest marches.

The biggest blunder, of course, took place in the bars.
Everyone within earshot suddenly became privy to their
drunken intel in the same way onlookers and passerbys can
see a post on Facebook without an account. When you're
slobbering drunk, you're far more likely to spill your guts

for bragging rights than to keep silent outright. Alcohol exaggerates truth much more than a lie.

Once a member outed himself publicly, it was like shooting fish in a barrel to identify the other underground members. In short, setting up a surveillance team to discover his comrades-in-arms and linking them to any IRA activity became dirt simple. And this was way before street cams or mobile phones became commonplace.

Offline Opsec

Once a link is known to law enforcement, the IRS or even the Mafia, they can sketch out a graph where they can pinpoint you or the rest of your group pretty quickly. Algorithms compute in light-speed, and the FBI even has algorithms that can fill in a 'family tree' of close ties and family, and can extrapolate data based on a person's online search parameters - and heaven help you if you're dumb enough to use the same cell phone or laptop you did before you ran. As well, your friend's behavior - where they eat, shop, shoot and sleep with - may aid in finding you. It's how the DEA map out drug rings like the cartels in Mexico or the Silk Road hidden Tor website; a site that went down in flames because the admin failed to employ good OPSEC.

The way to get around this for you, dear runner in Bangkok (other than zipping it in public and not dipping your pen in company ink) is to ensure no *cross-contamination* exists between those family tree branches (friends) vs. other neighboring trees. If you're on the run from Tony Soprano, for instance, you don't want your new Thai friend suddenly making friends with the new Sicilian in your building, a guy you know nothing about. He may just be Tony's nephew's best friend's golf partner. You never know. So sever that connection. As well, consider any contact by phone that links to your old associates contaminated.

Naturally this can apply to any country you're in, not just Thailand. But in Thailand, expats stick out more than one would in say, Ireland or the UK, so extra measures are required to stay 'dark' until the heat is off.

Online Opsec

We mentioned contamination for a good reason. If you're fresh off the Santa Maria, you need to lie low for a bit. If you must contact anyone from your 'old world', you must do so via a new computer or new phone. You cannot import any old world contacts from Facebook, either, since those are contaminated. Regardless if I'm in Phukit or Bangkok, here's what I would deploy if I had to stay off the radar for six months:

A new laptop with no cam (paid in cash), and absolutely no Google browsers!
VMware for Virtual Machines (VMs)
Linux/Ubuntu installed within VMware (no logs, with updates turned off)
Apps:
　Tor Browser

PGP for communicating incognito with NEW KEYS made, within the VM

No Windows - No Online Games, No non-Tor browsers, No Google

If you use this setup to talk to dear old mom back in California, it's a good bet that she's being monitored if you've stepped in some deep schnitzel. Consider a keylogger or pen device (eavesdropping for landlines) installed on her machine and is recording everything. Obviously, she cannot ever know that you're in Southeast Asia. It's also a good idea for her to use the same setup as you are. If your laptop is stolen or confiscated by the police, they can't link you to any activity on your device, nor can they decrypt your chat logs.

If you decide to chat with mom by video, you should know that things in the background like electrical sockets and furniture are often country-specific. They can give your location away fairly easily (like 'wall rugs in Russia and Ukraine). Thailand uses a very clever hybrid electrical socket which takes both round-pin European-style plugs and flat-pin North American-style plugs.

China

China's an immense country to get lost in. For anything incognito, its easier by a factor of 1000 compared to the USA. The bonus is that if you're dead set on running here, you won't have to worry about extradition treaties since mainland China has none with the U.S. This can save your life if you're a whistleblower like Edward Snowden, or someone connected to WikiLeaks. Hong Kong though, is another matter entirely.

The fine print is this: China can veto any extradition process if it interferes with defense or public policy. It's all a bit murky to be honest. On a technical level, yes, *Hong Kong* has an extradition treaty with the U.S., but that was before Great Britain gave control of Hong Kong over to the mainland. Snowden made it clear in an interview that he felt this was just too much of a grey area to risk staying in the country long term.

Disappearing Behind The Great Wall

This is easier said than done. Sure, it's easy to flee there, but it's hard to disappear in a way that makes you invisible to the Chinese. Very hard. in fact. Americans in China tend to acquire an affliction ten times quicker than even in the Philippines; an affliction called "Rock Star" affliction. That means mega attraction. If you're a 6'1 white guy then you'll get plenty of attraction in the Philippines. Guaranteed. But in China it's a whole other world of problems for someone wanting to go incognito, and once you've got it, it bonds to your ego like superglue. To state that it's difficult to peel yourself off the sticky crowd is an understatement. You may even like it when the crowed of kids start running their fingers through your hair in broad daylight.

You might be thinking, 'Well, I'm just an old ugly hermit and no one's going to bother.' And you'd be dead wrong. Even if you're as ugly as Ernie and Bert with a funny black tulip for hair, you'll still stick out like Big Bird. If you're the Dutch blonde hair/blue eyes variety, you'll be as visible as Big Bird would be traveling with those little green aliens from Toy Story. You'll feel like zealots are pulling you in every direction except the one you want to go in. It's quite the extra-terrestrial experience, let me tell you.

The picture taking is the most obvious threat to your cover. It's all very cute at first, but it'll quickly grate on your nerves as many Chinese will ask you some fairly innocuous questions that, if you oblige, may soon turn entrapping.

"Take picture of my baby?" one may ask. This'll be asked many times when you go out and about. Only after three or four of these in a day, you'll begin to suspect a conspiracy. Well, it sort of is when you experience it. They like your *white skin*, for starters. The Chinese as a whole are known for extreme racism at both ends of the spectrum.

You'll be spied on by teenage schoolgirls who'll spy on you while hoping their giggling girlfriends don't give them away as they twirl their Hello Kitty purses. More conservative areas may yield less obvious giggling (behind curtains instead of telephone poles), but the effect is the same: It's impossible to blend in without actually speaking Chinese and knowing Chinese culture *and* wearing some kind of disguise.

Then there's the endless inane questions that'll come out of nowhere. Hearing the same ones over and over is like watching C-Span for kicks. And they'll come from anyone and everyone. In Japan they call them "Gaijin lovers" (foreigner lovers), and these nice yet quirky and strange beings will come up to you in Tokyo and launch wave after wave of data mining questions.

- Is is true all Americans own Glock like John Wayne?

- Is Texas like Seinfeld?

- Do you have a beautiful wife yet? Our city offers you many pretty wives!

- Are alien UFO really in Nevada? (Don't tell them it's in New Mexico)

- You has rose tattoo like all Americans? You show it?

- You has Hells Angels in family? You show photos?

Hong Kong Rudeness

Rudeness is nothing new in megacities. When you factor in the negatives like smog, traffic, crowded streets and litter everywhere, it's perfectly logical that a few circuits may pop here and there due to all the stress. You can't fault everyone for it, for everyone has their own way of dealing with it. Only some deal with it by projecting it onto you. Even in New Orleans I'd watch from the streetcar near the French Quarter how easily the mules became agitated every time another out-of-towner wanted a joyride in the hundred degree heat. Few enjoyed that life hectic life.

However, Hong Kong takes it to an entirely new level, and I suspect their love of all things money has something to do with it. Hyper-capitalism is a double-edged sword, and with the underlying anti-free speech Communism run by the government, there's little in the way of religion to act as a buffer or release valve. So you get a lot of sidewalk Chinese bashing right into you, even pushing you out of the way so they can make more money. Consequences be damned.

When I say 'push', I mean literally *pushed*. Some will actually shove you on the sidewalks and think nothing of it. Forty somethings, cab drivers, teenagers. Five teenage girls will walk in front of you carrying on a tune and yet give you zero space to walk past them on the sidewalk. Meanwhile they're yapping along with their Hello Kitty outfit and dropping attitude like catty tomcats. Then there's the cabbies who'll run you over for a few dollars more and when you call them on it, they'll look at you like you're in the wrong.

It's not that *every* Chinese person is like this, of course, but many in Hong Kong are and they're the ones that spoil the whole batch. Why? Because money is their chief religion and your feelings come pretty much last on the totem pole of priorities for them. Call them on it publicly and you'll get *The Look*. That Look says they could care less who they've offended. If you're in they're way on the street, you're an obstacle to be removed on their way to the top. I saw this more times than I can count.

I know what you're thinking. You're thinking that it's no different than what we see in the West. New York is, after all, not known for it's politeness and Las Vegas wasn't built on the backs of winners. Other cities are the same way, cities like Chicago and San Francisco and Los Angeles. Except in Hong Kong, there's other things lurking under their skin besides street rudeness that'll draw attention to yourself.

The horking and spitting and public flatulence can really take you by surprise, but worse than this was the difficulty in finding a trash can. Anywhere. I began to wonder if I needed to rent one to pull along like a poodle on a leash.

By contrast, my friend and I'd been amazed at how clean everything in Japan was. Even back alleys were devoid of litter for the most part. The one black cat we saw had one eye and looked ancient, but well-fed. As it dug its claws into a garbage can, it did so with such a surgical precision that we instantly looked at each other and said the same thing: "Ninja cat." Even the alley cats knew not to spread trash around - though admittedly they probably lamented the lack of rat presence.

We laughed as we walked on in that big metropolis called Tokyo. Only the longer we walked the more we'd notice that everything was so ridiculously clean that we made it a game to name every excessively 'clean' movie we'd seen. Science fiction films, mostly. Logan's Run - the sci-fi mall movie where everything shined with such a moonscape white that to sneeze without a handkerchief brought angry stares.

I stopped and looked around. I thought of China and how vastly different it was. What would happen, I wondered, if one threw a banana peel down onto the pavement, or emptied a Smoothie onto the street like they do in Toronto or New Orleans during Mardi Gras? Surely it'd rub someone's Chocobo feathers the wrong way.

Since the age of five, the aftermath of the celebrity parades always rubbed me the wrong way. It never mattered which ones. Sandra Bullock in Endymion? Didn't matter. Harry Connick jr riding Rex? Didn't matter. Nor did it ever matter how jazzy and expensive the floats were. Despite the street cleaning machines afterward, they never quite cleaned up. And the smell, god. The smell! Red syrupy Hurricane drinks, voodoo dolls, and broken plastic spears everywhere.

We walked for maybe a mile and saw two other tourists. Women. One tall, one short. Montreal accents. We discussed asking them to accompany us to a bar. I stopped my friend as one of them threw a coke can near to a garbage can but missed. It fell behind it. This was close to the Squaresoft building near the Shinjuku ward - the mega company who designed such blockbusters as Final Fantasy, Dragon Quest and Kingdom Hearts. It was near the train station and very close to the Citigroup-Japan skyscraper and SoftBank.

It was also in full view of maybe a dozen Japanese business owners out having a break. The act came as a shock to them, like she'd slapped the Prime Minister or something or muttered a some voodoo heresy against Chocobo games. After came the hushed whispers, then the finger pointing and one yelled something in Japanese. Angry and sharp and pointy.

Now, we're no Japanese linguists, but it became obvious this was about to turn ugly unless those gals made amends quickly. Except they walked off like it was no big deal. After that, all eyes fell to us. We'd been handed the torch.

"Well??", their eyes seemed to say.

I walked up to retrieve the Coke can with the stuff gluing the webbing on my fingers. I ditched it, then wiped the sugary syrup off with a napkin I'd plucked from the can, but not before three old ladies from a cafe and one old fellow who seemed like the arcade change guy came out and rebuked us as well, one by one... and in loud, unmistakable English. They'd wrongly assumed the two gals were friends of ours.

I apologized for them. It was all I could do.

Only as we changed the subject, they'd switch us back to the garbage topic. We'd change it again and ask where the cherry blossoms park was - and they'd lasso us back to those two litter-lizards like we were stubborn cattle. As far as they saw it, we were the guilty party because we'd stayed silent. So pay up, their eyes said. I went for my wallet to buy their silence when one touched my wrist. He shook his head. For a moment there I'd thought he was about to slice it off.

Only he didn't. He explained that Japanese love foreigners, and they want as many visitors as possible to come and experience Japan. and so it is for this reason that their streets are sparkling clean and subways immaculate. He also said that staying silent when you see an injustice is intolerable in Japan. We praised them, apologized, and left.

But back in China? It's a 180 degree turn into another dimension.

My friend relayed what he'd seen once on a Wednesday at a high-end Chinese restaurant. The waiter, who was obviously nursing a hangover, applied every other ice cold drink to his forehead in between taking orders when suddenly, he horked his lunch all over the floor. It was a putrid mess!

I know, I know, there's nothing unusual about that. Only after cleaning it up, this waiter doesn't bother to go to the restroom to wash up. He simply takes a mop to the floor, pushes the bucket back into the corner of the place, and resumed taking orders with the same filthy hands he'd horked with.

If you guessed that all of this negative attention can destroy your anonymity, you're right. And if you guessed that it can make you enemies in a land of opposites and anomalies, you're right again. The way to preserve your anonymity in such a land is to go with the flow. Don't ruffle feathers like we did in Japan. To be sure, that was just an experiment, and on that specific occasion what struck us as a double whammy was how polite those Japanese were when we politely explained what the heck we were doing.

But you're playing Russian roulette if you expect that same level of politeness in Hong Kong.

Counterfeiting

A short word on counterfeiting.

Counterfeited products are sold everywhere in China. You'll see various levels of it in the malls of China and even in the Philippines. Cheap shirts that rip into shreds in two weeks. Cheap Chinese electronics (phones, tablets) that break within two months. Iphones that aren't Iphones. Hard drives that seem to have been made from twigs and fish bones that croak after a week of use.

Souvenirs are hit and miss, too. You'll see items sold in antique stores that cost far below what they'd really sell for if they were even 10% authentic. Statuettes fall into this category and it's easy to get suckered. I was. They know how to replicate the look and feel of something old, dusty, archaic and webby, and since you can't speak Chinese, it's harder to detect a lie. They may charge you $100 for a vase that they claim is 8th century China, but if that's the case then the price would be closer to *ten grand*. This goes on all over China, where counterfeit goods fool thousands of naive visitors every year. If you're going drop major cash on a statue, first ensure it's appraised by someone you trust *before* laying your cash on the counter.

The Final Disappearing Act

As you can imagine, the cameras all over China generally seem to point in your direction. It can be a real headache for anonymity seekers, where a disguise may prove embarrassing (and possibly attract the attention of law enforcement) if your mustache falls off in front of a crowd of gawking Chinese.

"Is he a spy?"

"Why did he dye his hair?"

"Why does she wear a wig?"

"I will tell someone important about this huckster. Get a reward!"

Nevertheless, here are some things that have helped me whenever that 'Stranger in a Strange Land' feeling came around.

I.) <u>Learn a basic level of Chinese</u>. Do this, and they may forgive just about anything you do short of stealing nuclear launch codes. Like Thailand, you cannot travel incognito without it anyway, so you need to learn the basics of how to get around. Basics like:

How to rent cars, hotels, how to read maps to get to a bank so you can open a savings account. Even ordering a nice steak at a restaurant requires some rudimentary Chinese.

You must also understand Chinese culture on a deep level. It isn't rude for them to say "You're getting fat!" like it is in America. It's like saying, "You're a little sunburned" to someone in Florida. But it is *very* rude for a Chinese woman on a subway to mutter "hei gue" (black devil) to you if you're black. You can call her out for it.

If you do, chances are good her eyes will well up with tears and she'll beg for your forgiveness.

II.) <u>Rock Star Status</u> gets stale after a good while, believe it or not. Read any interview with Steven Tyler or Garth Brooks and you'll see that even those heavyweights grow weary of all that attention, as will you. To that, don't assume that since everyone is taking *your* picture that it's okay to take everyone *else's* picture.

III.) <u>Talk With Your Hands</u> - If you don't speak Chinese, don't shoot a pic of a local Chinese guy without doing some sign language to ask first. As in, point to him, then to the camera, then ask with your eyebrows.

IV.) <u>Be assertive and say NO</u> when necessary. Learn how to say it in Mandarin and learn not to worry about hurting their feelings. Some Chinese students once asked to snap a picture of me because I am 6'2 and have vampire-white skin. This was just outside the French Quarter near the St. Louis Cathedral. I calmly told them my vampire clan would be upset if they ever found out I was walking around in the daytime, since technically it was against the clan's rules. They'd likely come after who shot the picture. Their eyes grew as big as dinner plates.

"Vampires?" they asked, just as a flurry of flashes went off.

Final Thoughts

When all is said and done, you may believe that the disappearing act is just not your forte. That it's just not in you. That it's something for other men to grapple with. Houdini's grandkids, even. After all, they're certainly primed to all the buttery grace their father exhibited, and then some. But you? Naw. That's too high a tightrope act for your troupe. And you're no acrobat, right?

Well, not really. Houdini was only well-known because he took that all-important first step on the highwire.

Listen, if you've read this far, then that means you're smarter than 80% of the other guys who quit reading back in Chapter 3. Those guys are the Doubting Thomas's who told Houdini he was a fool. Who told him that he was wasting his time setting his sights so high. And I'll tell you something. Those guys are cut from the same cloth as St. Thomas himself, the same who'd demanded to see the scars on His hands before he'd believe. Guys like that won't take action until fire is raining down from the sky. Only then will they cower in the corner as lava enters their home, thinking they may not get burned if they only cower in a corner like a mouse nibbling on his last morsel of cheese.

Or they'll say to themselves, "I've got too much to lose. I could lose my house for crying out loud. My house! Then there's my family, my dog, my cat, my loans, my cycle," ad nauseum.

Problem is, they're wrong. Those things will make a slave of you if you allow it. So don't allow it! Don't be one of them. Don't end up as one of the men who live under a bridge in Bunkie, LA with a 2% city unemployment rate and still make excuses why they didn't take action when they had the chance. Take a risk. The details always work themselves out.

The NSA, along with about 100 other alphabet agencies around the world, are now focused on making criminals out of those innocent law abiders who are slaves to the system. Pre-crime is what they create. And you won't be spared short of a revolution, either. Sooner or later, your number will turn up.

You probably have more questions now than when you began this journey. Questions like,

How much in the way of resources does one man need to start over?

How much money? Chinese connections? Thai? How many players? How many prayers and hail Marys and rosary beads do I need to rub? How many dyed lucky rabbit's feet keychains?

The truth is you don't need to be John Rambo to disappear when the going gets rough, nor do you need to survive a manhunt in a Washington forest and survive an abandoned mine shaft with nothing but a Bowie knife to slice up things that'd make a billy goat puke. All it takes, believe it or not, is a little intestinal fortitude. Also known as *balls*. That elusive ability to ignore pain, lightning, and brave the storm and get that stubborn engine started to zoom away out of danger. Most men don't have it. Most Marines do, but you don't have to be one of those guys either.

As for what resources you need, it depends.

Whenever I hear that question, usually the person's looking for an excuse not to act. An excuse to stay in their 'safe' job, also known as The Cubicle.

But on the whole, I'd say the amount of resources depend on how invisible you want to be. It's a whole other ball game for Mary out in Alaska than it is for Jo Beth in the Bayou of Louisiana. There's levels to it with accordant risk vs. reward built into any escape plan. Little league ain't the NFL and Lucky Dogs (those hot dog stands in the French Quarter) aren't culinary delights from Paris. People have cultural standards and expectations. People make mistakes when they don't change. Big ones. Can you recover from a big one you might make someday?

Example: You may be invisible one day in Canada but make a major goof the next. Then your Newfoundland friends'll wonder why you kept saying 'who dat?' after a few beers at the sports bar. They'll especially sniff you out if you prattle on about your dog's awesome day on the Krewe of Barkus as it rolled on Fat Tuesday. The next morning, you may not remember it. But they will. Can you recover from it?

They may even investigate further, and since invisibility is a power few people can wield effectively, they'll want to know what your secret magic sauce is just as surely as if you walked into the bar wearing a green beret. They'll ask, "How'd you get away with it for so long? Who you runnin' from? The FBI? Interpol? Jabba the Hutt?"

They may even pressure you into giving up the goods in a public setting. Like a bar. With everyone watching. Can you recover from it?

The point here isn't to scare you *from* taking action. The point is to scare you *into* taking action. It's to convince you that you'll never learn to get really good at something unless you take action and learn from your mistakes. Risk vs. Reward. Brains over brawn. Recall what General Patton said to his troops:

"The quicker we clean up this mess, the quicker we can take a little jaunt against the purple pissing Japs and clean out their nest, too... before the goddamned Marines get all of the credit!"

If you don't deal with a mess when it falls into your lap, the mess will grow bigger until there's nothing left for you to do but wave a white flag of surrender as it engulfs you completely. Remember what we discussed about stalkers? Make as much noise as possible. Get mad. Take massive action. Worry not about tomorrow, a wise man once said.

Another example. Forget about stalking ex-lovers for a moment. Let's say you're on the run from the **authorities**. If you can master that, you can master anything because it becomes a hundred times harder if you now have not one, but *dozens* of professional stalkers who are trained to find people on the run.

Knowing what the authorities greatest strengths and weaknesses are can help you out since many get cocky and overconfident after years of success. They get to the point where they think they can do anything. To anyone. At any time. That's because the taxpayer always pays for their mistakes one way or another. This is in your favor because it's a weakness you can exploit. But you have to ask the right questions and set up a Plan B, a Plan C, etc. before you run. In other words, take action. Assume risk. Don't worry about next week. See a pattern here?

Questions you need to ask yourself are:

Can they monitor every train station? Bus depots? Can they shut them down with a court order on the fly? A few can post-9/11, but which ones? You find this out by calling the low-totem guys who work there day in, day out. Not the FBI.

How about gas stations - how many have cameras? Which ones don't? Are there payphones you can use to verify which ones? Underground tunnels; can they seal you tight by closing off both ends? You must know all of this before running.

All of the preceding questions is what a man on the run from the authorities needs to know beforehand. Are you a man on the run? If not, why are you not taking action?

Let's go a little farther with that 'man on the run from authorities' example.

ID

Most men on the run from the law don't bother with this. They don't plan ahead. ID can be a pain in the neck even if you're *not* in trouble. There's a world of difference between showing a fake ID to a bank to open an account and one that'll get you past airport security. So you'll need a fake passport, and yes, they're expensive. More than a grand in most cities, and you must ensure your contact isn't a cop.

Do you plan on hoofing it by foot, or hitchhiking? This brings a whole new level of risk since you'll stick out even more than you're already sticking out. You'll be a stick in the mud wearing one of those twirly caps.

Besides, hitchhiking hasn't gotten any safer these days. Think about it. How many hitchhikers did you see last week? If you live near Yosemite or the Appalachian trail, I'll grant maybe thirty or so. Anywhere else, not so many. Better to rent a car, but be picky about it and find a small rental outlet that accepts cash deposits. Know that whatever identification you use will be used to run a credit check. That's more risk.

Sanctuary: Go somewhere where American tourists and expats are few and far between. You need not go to Yemen, but consider South America, which is filled with nice little getaways to allow the heat to simmer down. Mexico is a bit too close for comfort (though Yucatan is a nice spot). Many go to Venezuela, but you don't want to stay there forever. Can your parents visit you? Should they, if they're being watched?

Funds

You run out of money quickly being on the run, so you needs lots of it. Enough to bankroll your hotels as well as gasoline for travel and, let's face it, you don't want to eat Thai food 365 days a year. I'd say save at least five years worth as this'll buy more than you can imagine. That brings up our next topic: Friends.

Friends

There's a saying in Hong Kong about money: *"When money is stolen, you can only beat the dog."*

Put another way, if you have money, you have *friends*. It's a rather Nietzschian way to view things but it is what it is. And those same friends will help you out in a jam, one that'll come sooner than later. The difference could be whether you sleep in a nice air-conditioned house far away from the authorities, or in a cell in Nowhereville where the mice race over your ankles next to the splayed legs of Soapy the wino. You'll wish you'd saved more money at that point.

The above is overkill for 90% of the people in trouble. Which category do you fall in? Are you waiting for everything to be perfect before you leave the sinking ship? Let me give one final bit of advice, then I'll shut up.

Don't wait until marshal law is declared. Don't wait until e-verify backfires and we're all corralled like sheep to the bloody slaughter. Don't wait until the NSA is granted even more power by unelected officials. Get out there. Now. Learn how to travel internationally. Learn how other people in other countries with different cultures and problems and climates disappear. Pay them to teach you. A hundred bucks over there is like a thousand here.

Learn how to live anonymous now, online *and* offline, while you still have time and freedom on your side.

Remember, lady luck favors the prepared.

Godspeed, and may you be judged by the strength of your enemies!

Would You Like to Know More?

First off, I owe you a big thanks and a round of the best German beer money can buy. You could've picked any one of dozens of great books on this topic and you took a chance with mine. So, thank you for that. Seriously. Working through to the end takes a strong mind and the patience of a saint, especially where invisibility is concerned. If you liked what you heard then I need your help. Please take a moment to leave a review for this book so others can learn to protect themselves.

If you're interested, here are my other works. These books solve *problems* people have.

Tor and the Dark Art of Anonymity
Darknet: A Guide to Staying Anonymous Online (Audio & Kindle)
Usenet and the Future of Anonymity
Anonymous File Sharing: How to Be a Ghost in the Machine
Social Media in an Anti-Social World
Cell Anonymity: How to Be Anonymous on Android, Blackberry and Apple

Made in the USA
Monee, IL
26 December 2021